Frances Tenenbaum, Series Editor

HOUGHTON MIFFLIN COMPANY
Boston • New York 1998

Kitchen Gardens

How to create a beautiful and functional culinary garden

CATHY WILKINSON BARASH

For information about permission to reproduce selections from this book,
write to Permissions, Houghton Mifflin Company, 215 Park Avenue South,
New York, New York 10003.

Taylor's Guide is a registered trademark of Houghton Mifflin Company.

Library of Congress Cataloging-in-Publication Data

Barash, Cathy Wilkinson, date.
    Kitchen gardens / Cathy Wilkinson Barash.
      p.   cm. — (Taylor's weekend gardening guides)
    Includes index.
    ISBN 0-395-82749-3
    1. Vegetable gardening. 2. Organic gardening. 3. Kitchen gardens.
    I. Title. II. Series.
    SB324.3.B37 1998
    635—dc21   98–11771

Printed in the United States of America.

WCT 10 9 8 7 6 5 4 3 2 1

Book design by Deborah Fillion
Drawings by Elayne Sears
Cover photograph © by Cathy Wilkinson Barash

CONTENTS

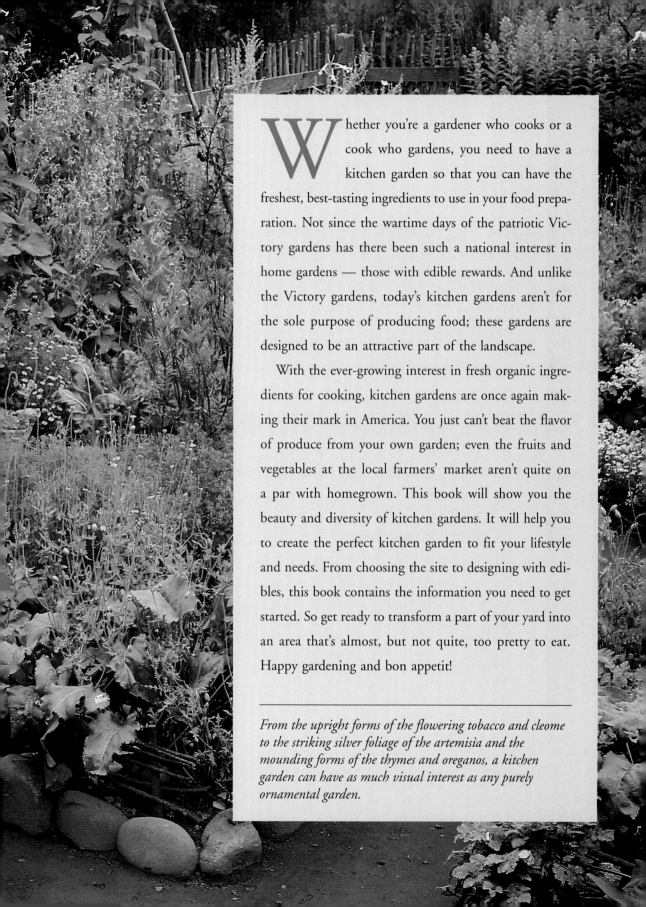

Whether you're a gardener who cooks or a cook who gardens, you need to have a kitchen garden so that you can have the freshest, best-tasting ingredients to use in your food preparation. Not since the wartime days of the patriotic Victory gardens has there been such a national interest in home gardens — those with edible rewards. And unlike the Victory gardens, today's kitchen gardens aren't for the sole purpose of producing food; these gardens are designed to be an attractive part of the landscape.

With the ever-growing interest in fresh organic ingredients for cooking, kitchen gardens are once again making their mark in America. You just can't beat the flavor of produce from your own garden; even the fruits and vegetables at the local farmers' market aren't quite on a par with homegrown. This book will show you the beauty and diversity of kitchen gardens. It will help you to create the perfect kitchen garden to fit your lifestyle and needs. From choosing the site to designing with edibles, this book contains the information you need to get started. So get ready to transform a part of your yard into an area that's almost, but not quite, too pretty to eat. Happy gardening and bon appetit!

From the upright forms of the flowering tobacco and cleome to the striking silver foliage of the artemisia and the mounding forms of the thymes and oreganos, a kitchen garden can have as much visual interest as any purely ornamental garden.

Chapter 1

The Kitchen Garden, Past and Present

A kitchen garden is, by definition, a garden that is sited near the culinary center of the house and provides the fruits and vegetables for the household. It usually contains those ingredients that are best when fresh-picked, at their peak of ripeness, and used immediately, preferably at the next meal. Historically, many kitchen gardens produced all the vegetables — those that were eaten fresh as well as those that were to be put up for out-of-season use. Potager is the French term for kitchen garden, and it often denotes a formal, geometric, edible garden.

A kitchen garden need not be limited to vegetables; it can include fruits, herbs, and edible flowers. It is restricted only by the space the gardener has and the plants that he or she desires. It can range from a small culinary herb garden that includes a few basic herbs, such as parsley, rosemary, sage, thyme, basil, and oregano, to a large, 50- by 100-foot vegetable garden that feeds a family of six, to one that encompasses acres, just like some of the old European estate kitchen gardens do.

The hand-wrought twig fence combined with the red-shingled shed set the scene for a bucolic kitchen garden in upstate New York.

Kitchen gardens have always played an important role in the landscape. The pleasure gardens of the ancient Middle East were as practical as they were beautiful. They were walled gardens that were not only private spaces; the walls kept the gardens warm, so all sorts of exotic fruits and vegetables could be grown within their shelter. There was often a pool in the center of the garden. The fish in the pool were also functional; they were often served for a meal after they had been admired glinting in the water. In the Middle Ages the first true kitchen gardens emerged — these were the herb gardens of the monasteries. Not only did this mark the introduction of the kitchen garden, it was also the beginning of the isolation of edibles from the rest of the landscape, a practice that has continued until this century.

Traditionally such a garden was an enclosed, symmetrical, four-square design with two central paths that ran perpendicular to one another, intersecting in the middle of the garden, thus effectively dividing the garden into four equal parts. Often a well or a spring was at the center, eliminating the need for carrying water

The raised bed of the boxed salad garden warms up faster than surrounding soil, allowing for a bountiful crop of greens early in summer, even as far north as Vermont.

Rosemary Verey's potager at Barnsley House in England was based on the formal gardens at Villandry. Trained fruit trees add to the formal aspect of the garden.

great distances to irrigate the garden. Each square was divided into various raised beds, delineated by permanent paths. Even the simplest design usually included a perimeter bed surrounded by an enclosure of some sort — a wall or tall hedge. These were efficient gardens planted with a range of fruits, vegetables, and herbs. The diversity of plant material grown did not tax the soil the way a monoculture of a single crop would. And it kept the rest of the life of the garden in balance, attracting a diversity of birds, insects, and other small creatures that helped keep pests in check.

In the 18th and 19th centuries, the French made kitchen gardens into a high art form, as evidenced by the geometric potagers, such as the garden at Villandry, that are still growing today. Intricate curves were added to the garden, and beds were formally edged, often with evergreen and perennial herbs, such as boxwood

A modified picket fence gives a traditional American feel to this suburban Virginia kitchen garden. Although it is contemporary, it looks as if it could be a colonial garden.

or germander, that gave the garden interest off-season as well. Plants were trained to grow over arbors, pergolas, and trellises. Fruits were espaliered and cordoned, adding to the formal majesty of these gardens. The gardens grew in size in proportion with the owner's wealth — a nobleman's potager might be as large as ten acres. These gardens were often surrounded by a brick or stone wall, which had the added advantage of tempering the climate within the garden, allowing more tender fruits and vegetables to be grown.

In rural colonial America the kitchen garden was the mainstay of the household — the main garden from which a range of produce was harvested, as opposed to the large fields of single crops that were cultivated for commerce.

The vegetable garden at Monticello is planted today much as it was in Jefferson's time, using a variety of heirloom vegetables, fruits, and flowers.

These gardens were much more practical and less formal than their European predecessors while keeping the basic four-square design with its inherent efficiency and practicality.

Thomas Jefferson's kitchen garden at Monticello is one of the best-known historic American kitchen gardens. In a scant 1,000 feet by 80 feet he grew some 250 varieties of vegetables and herbs. A master of edible landscaping — some two hundred years before it was even called that — Jefferson designed his kitchen garden to be aesthetically pleasing as well as immensely practical, using colorful vegetables for their beauty as a part of the design.

At Mount Vernon, George Washington had an impressive kitchen garden

The kitchen gardens at Williamsburg are planted in the same manner today as they were three hundred years ago. Originally they provided all the herbs and vegetables for the family.

that preserved some of the European formality. It is maintained today with many of the same plants that Washington grew. There is a wall on only one side of the garden, which helps to protect and warm the espaliered plants below. Dwarf apples and pears are cordoned, making unique 2- to 3-foot-high edges to some of the beds. Herbs, such as lavender, rosemary, and thyme, are used as edges for other beds. Washington was ahead of his time, composting kitchen waste as well as animal waste to incorporate into the garden soil. He even located the main outhouse on the other side of the garden wall (from a distance it looks like a handsome gazebo). A removable drawer slightly above ground level allowed liquids to seep into the soil while solid material could be easily removed and mixed into the compost piles.

The kitchen garden in America is continuing to evolve, with gardeners in different parts of the country adapting the garden design to suit their needs and habitats. Still, the basic tenets of multiple raised beds, some type of enclosure, and proximity to the house and water remain to this day. And, because of the types of plants grown, these gardens by necessity are located in a sunny spot. Within these pages you'll see a range of gardens, large to small, that will inspire you to create your own kitchen garden.

The exuberance of a kitchen garden is evident in the lush squash leaves, under which lies a bountiful harvest.

CHAPTER 2

GET GROWING, FROM THE GROUND UP

Good soil is essential for a bountiful kitchen garden. An advantage that you have in creating a kitchen garden for the first time is that such gardens are traditionally made from raised beds. Then, even if your soil is not as good as it should be, you can build it up (literally and figuratively) by adding plenty of organic matter in the form of compost, well-rotted manure, or leaf mold (the remains of a leaf pile that has decayed over several years). Before you get started working in your kitchen garden, it helps to know a bit about the ground you're going to be planting.

SOIL BASICS

Most gardeners don't call it dirt (dirt is what gets under your fingernails after a day of working in the garden); they call it soil. That's because soil is a living substance with a variety of biological, chemical, and physical forces that are con-

Planted in hills in the garden bed, the squashes are allowed to cover the ground, successfully shading out weeds. A small, hard-packed dirt path allows access to the cutting flowers and the lean-to greenhouse.

stantly at work. Soil is made up of five major components: air, living organisms (from microscopic bacteria, viruses, and fungi to larger earthworms and insects), humus (organic material in varying states of decay), water, and inorganic particles of minerals and rocks.

The Types of Soil

There are three basic soil types — sand, silt, and clay — determined by the size of the inorganic particles. It isn't common to see a pure soil of any type; most garden soil is a mixture of the three. Although laboratory testing can determine your exact soil composition, most gardeners can figure out the type of soil they have pretty easily.

Gently squeeze a small amount of soil in your hand, then rub it between your fingers. Sandy soil is composed of the largest particles and feels gritty to the touch. It does not stay together when squeezed. Sandy soil is easy to work and it drains very well. However, the water draining through it removes most of the nutrients as it goes. Clay (also known as heavy soil) absorbs and holds a tremendous amount of moisture. It is very smooth, almost silky to the touch. Its particles are so fine that it holds its shape when squeezed or compressed, which does not allow for air or water movement within the soil. Silt particles are halfway between sand and clay in size; silt has a smooth texture. It can be squeezed together and does not remain compacted, especially when dry. Good garden soil is called loam and is a mixture of silt, sand, and clay. When you rub it between your fingers, it breaks up into smaller particles. Loam holds moisture well and has enough organic matter to encourage the biological activity that is necessary for healthy soil.

Amending the Soil

Soil is the major source of food and water for the plants in your garden. Thus, it is important to take the time to choose a proper location and prepare the soil well before you plant. The most vigorous tomato, if planted in poor soil, will not thrive or produce much fruit. Conversely, even a tomato that has been left in a small container too long will flourish if planted in good soil that is enriched with lots of organic matter. The three characteristics of good soil are good drainage, plenty of humus, and an abundance of nutrients available to the plant.

Quick Soil Type Test

Another way to determine the type of soil you have is to mix about half a cup of your topsoil with a cup and a half of water in a covered jar. Shake well to break up the soil; let it sit overnight. The various components will settle out and the proportions will indicate the type of soil. Sand, with the largest particles, settles to the bottom with silt on top of it and clay on top of the silt. If the layer of silt is the same size as the layers of clay and sand, you have a good loam. If the proportion of sand is slightly greater than the silt and clay, it's a sandy loam; if clay is greater than silt and sand (with those two amounts equal), it's clayey loam.

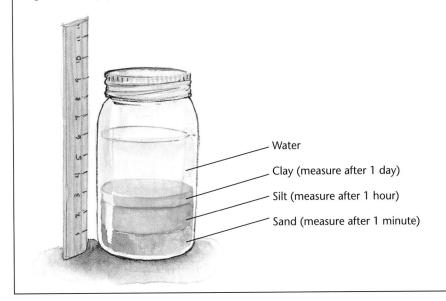

Water

Clay (measure after 1 day)

Silt (measure after 1 hour)

Sand (measure after 1 minute)

When you're starting out, it is worth the time and effort to improve the soil in each bed before you plant. More than most plants, vegetables and fruits require a lot of nutrition from the soil, so you need to replace the missing nutrients. This is best done by side-dressing extra-hungry plants with compost or adding several inches of compost to the entire bed each spring or fall.

All soil can benefit from the addition of organic material. Turn the soil, breaking up any large clods. For every 100 square feet of soil, add about 2 pounds of rock phosphate (ground-up rocks), 2 pounds of granite meal, and 10 to 15 pounds of compost, well-rotted manure, or leaf mold. Turn this into the soil and dig it in well. It's best to prepare a new bed in fall so you're ready to plant in spring.

pH: Acidity and Alkalinity

pH is the measurement of relative acidity and alkalinity, measured on a scale of 0 to 14, with 0 the most acidic, 14 the most alkaline, and 7 neutral. Most fruits and vegetables prefer a slightly acid soil, with the pH about 6.5. The main exceptions are blueberries, which demand a much more acid soil, about 4.5. If the soil pH is not right for a particular plant, it cannot get the nutrients it needs from the soil. If you amend the soil well before planting, it is not necessary to worry about soil pH when planting in subsequent years.

When first starting a garden, it's a good idea to check the pH, especially if you live in an area where you know the soil tends to be either very acid or alkaline. Although you can send your soil to a laboratory for testing, it is not always necessary. Simple kits for testing pH are available at most nurseries and garden centers. Many nurseries will offer pH testing free (or at a nominal fee) for their customers. Your local Cooperative Extension Service also offers pH testing.

If you're planning your kitchen garden near an old house, it would be wise to have the soil tested for lead, which can be a contaminant from old paint scrapings. This is especially important if you have young children who will be eating the produce from the garden. If the soil tests positive for lead, you may have to have it taken away by a professional who is licensed to properly dispose of contaminated soil.

Once you have determined the pH of the soil, see how it matches up to the ideal pH for the plants you plan to grow. Unless the pH is way off one way or the other, you can opt just to amend it with organic matter. Although you may not grow blue-ribbon quality veggies, they'll be good enough. You'll still enjoy them.

However, if the soil is extremely alkaline, you'll need to add elemental sulfur (apply according to package directions) to get the pH closer to neutral (in essence, you're making the soil more acid). If it is too acid, add dolomitic limestone to make it sweeter. The soil pH will not change overnight with addition

In fall, simple paths are made by laying moistened newspaper (10 sheets thick) on top of the soil. The paper is then covered with leaves, which will decompose over the winter and can be raked up onto the beds in spring.

of these materials; that's why it's best to amend the soil in fall, in preparation for a spring planting.

To Till or Not to Till

For years gardeners were encouraged to grow vegetables in fenced-in gardens with all the plants in neat rows. They were told to double-dig the beds, a technique that involves back-breaking labor, digging down 2 feet deep and turning all the soil. And each spring they were urged to till the entire garden before planting. I never subscribed to this school of gardening; for one thing it's too much work.

Today's gardeners are looking to less labor-intensive methods. Recent studies have shown that repeated tilling of the soil does not improve it. Instead, tilling brings weed seeds, which have lain dormant far below the soil surface, up to a level where they can germinate, making more work for the gardener in the form of extra weeding. Research also points out that in soil that is not mulched, the top $\frac{1}{4}$ to $\frac{1}{2}$ inch of the soil is virtually dead, containing none of the myriad flora and fauna that thrive just a fraction of an inch lower. The top layer of the soil has been sterilized by the sun. Thus, when you till, not only do you move the dead soil down into the fertile area, you move live soil to the top where, in time, the sun will kill any living organisms in it. It is much more logical — and less work — to leave the soil alone and simply mulch it to protect the delicate balance of life within.

MULCH: NOT JUST A PRETTY DRESSING

After taking care of the soil — remember you are feeding the soil, not the plant — the second most important key to a successful kitchen garden is mulch. Organic mulch, laid several inches thick, not only helps eliminate weeds by smothering the young seeds, it also conserves water by cutting down on the moisture that is lost through evaporation. Mulch also helps to keep the soil temperature more constant. And the added benefit of using an organic mulch (as opposed to an inorganic mulch like plastic, stones, sand, or gravel) is that it eventually breaks down and adds humus to the soil. Thus, it improves the soil structure and provides nutrients for your plants. As the lower layer of mulch becomes part of the soil, a new layer of mulch has to be added, usually in the fall. I also mulch in the spring, a couple of weeks after major planting. Be sure to keep

Organic Mulches

Choose from these mulches to keep weeds at bay and conserve water in your garden.

Buckwheat hulls (they have a tendency to blow around in a windy area)

Chopped leaves (run them over with your lawnmower several times, otherwise they'll clump and not let moisture through to the soil)

Cocoa hulls

Grass clippings (never apply more than 1 inch of fresh clippings at a time)

Ground corn cobs

Newspaper (black ink only — this is best laid down in dampened layers about 8 to 10 sheets thick, then covered with a thin layer of a more decorative mulch)

Peanut hulls

Pecan hulls

Pine needles (pine straw)

Salt hay (use what washes up on the beach; if you cut the hay, you risk destroying part of the beach's ecology)

Sawdust (light color may not be attractive; contrary to popular belief, sawdust will not rob nitrogen from the soil)

Shredded bark

Straw

Wood shavings

mulch at least an inch from stems and trunks of plants. If the mulch is piled right next to young transplants, you could bury them and encourage insects, bacteria, fungi, and viruses to enter the tender stems. I add more mulch in the middle of the growing season, especially if it is warm and wet.

You have a large choice of organic mulch materials. However, not all are available in every part of the country. The material you use for mulch is a personal choice. Some mulches, such as cocoa or buckwheat hulls, give a more formal look, while others, such as pine straw or salt hay, look more rustic. Some mulches may be free while others are pricey, which may be a consideration if you have a large garden to mulch. It's a good idea to add some nitrogen-rich fertil-

A mulch of hay or straw serves two purposes: it effectively smothers weeds and weed seeds while maintaining soil moisture and temperature.

izer to the soil when mulching (especially if you're using sawdust, pine needles, bark, or leaves) to keep the carbon-nitrogen ratio of the soil in balance.

Recently I've been using paper from my office, run through a shredder, as a mulch. I moisten it and cover it with a thin layer of compost and then cover it all over with pine needles or shredded bark. Within a year, the paper has broken down and added nutrients to my soil, instead of taking up space in some already overcrowded landfill. I now happily shred any black and white (non-glossy) junk mail and add it to my garden. When the paper supply is too large, I put the shreddings in the compost pile in a layer no thicker than 6 inches.

COMPOST: BLACK GOLD

Unfortunately, there has been so much written about the "science" of composting that it has turned many gardeners off. What percentage of brown to green, different types of bins, anaerobic and aerobic bacteria — it even sounds confusing. Basically, if you leave any organic matter long enough, it will rot. That is what composting is all about — rotting.

Composting Basics

Composting can be as simple or complex as you wish. You don't need anything fancy, just something to contain the compost and keep it in a vertical pile. You can use chicken or turkey wire shaped into a 36-square-inch box (this seems to be the magic size for optimum composting), or a 36-inch-diameter cylinder. Fancy composters can cost hundreds of dollars, or you can make one from wooden pallets, which are available free at many large stores. Use one pallet for the base, then wire three together to form the sides. Leave the front open or hinge a fifth pallet on one side for easier access.

There are three requirements for decomposition — air, water, and microorganisms. Air is plentiful, unless you are composting in one of the sealed plastic composting bins. Some gardeners have had good results with them, but I have had problems with malodorous compost — usually a sign of anaerobic rather than aerobic decomposition — using this type of composter. With a closed composter, you also have to make sure to water it. With open bins, unless there is extreme drought, moisture from the material added to the bin and rainfall provide sufficient moisture. The microorganisms come from the soil — you need to start with some good garden soil and add an inch or so to every 6 or 8 inches of compostable material as you put it on the pile.

Start your compost pile by putting a couple of inches of soil — the richest you have, filled with worms and all those invisible, hungry microorganisms — at the bottom. Then add the small weeds you pull up (no weeds in seed, please, and none of the invasive running weeds), cuttings from the garden (no material larger than half an inch in diameter; larger items take too long to break down — make a separate brush pile for them), shredded leaves (you can run over them with a lawnmower first, especially very large leaves, which can mat together), grass clippings (no more than an inch at a time or they slime and nothing gets through them), all the kitchen garbage except animal products (coffee grounds and the cof-

This three-bin composting system is elegant, with a pergola overhead for annual vines such as 'Scarlet Runner' or hyacinth beans to climb on.

fee filter paper, vegetable peelings, eggshells — these are the one exception to the animal products rule), including the moldy zucchini in the vegetable drawer, the sprouted and green potatoes in the bin, leftovers from dinner (no veggies or salads with oil or butter on them for the compost) — you get the idea. Sprinkle in a handful of lime when you start the pile. Lightly water the pile initially. After that, you may need to water it every week or two if there is no rain and if the material you add to it is dry. As you accumulate material, just add it to the pile.

For the best compost, combine dried (brown) material, such as autumn leaves, with fresh (green) matter, such as trimmings from the garden, grass clippings, and vegetable kitchen waste.

You may get to feel like I do — much less guilty about throwing out food if it's going back to feed the soil as compost. I prefer to have two bins. When the first is filled, I start on the second bin. By the time the second one is filled, the material in the first bin has broken down into compost — rich, dark brown matter that will feed the soil, which in turn nourishes your plants. Black gold is what gardeners call it. Like alchemists, we are able to turn worthless garbage into a valuable resource for the garden, with no muss and no fuss.

FERTILIZERS

There are times when you may have to add fertilizers to the soil. Your own soil may become depleted or there may be a particular plant that's a very heavy feeder and the soil may need a nutrient boost. As you look at the shelves of fertilizers, it is easy to become confused. Which is best? What do the numbers on the packages mean? Does a bigger number mean a better fertilizer?

N-P-K: The Numbers

When you look at any package of fertilizer, whether it is organic or synthetic, there are three numbers, separated by dashes, such as 2-3-3, 5-10-5, or 20-20-20. These numbers denote the N-P-K ratio of the fertilizer and represent the percentage of nitrogen (N), phosphorus (P), and potassium (K) in the fertilizer. These are the main elements that a plant needs (macronutrients). Nitrogen promotes leaf growth; phosphorus fosters strong roots, hastens maturation, and is essential for fruit and seed development; and potassium, also known as potash, is necessary for cell division in buds and roots.

What are the best ways to amend the soil to provide good nutrition for your fruits and vegetables? The organic choices give you the nutrients you seek, in a form that is taken up slowly by the plant rather than the quick fix of most synthetic fertilizers. Nitrogen is readily available in blood meal, cottonseed meal, fish meal, and fish emulsion. Milorganite, activated sewage sludge from the city of Milwaukee, has been available commercially for decades and is a good source of nitrogen. Extensive testing has shown that there is no heavy metal contamination, so it is safe for edibles. Bone meal and rock phosphate are good sources of phosphorus. The best sources of potassium are hardwood ash and granite dust. Dig banana skins directly into the ground (a process known as sheet composting) for a good boost of potassium. Stephen Scanniello, the rosarian at Brooklyn Botanic Garden, eats two bananas a day and feeds the skins to his roses. He claims that the roses have flourished since the addition of banana skins to their diet.

It's helpful to know that some plants are much more demanding of certain soil nutrients than others. Many of the leafy green vegetables, such as chicory, lettuce, spinach, and most other salad greens, require a lot of nitrogen to keep producing leaves. The brassicas, members of the mustard family such as broccoli, cauliflower, kale, cabbage, Brussels sprouts, and kohlrabi also require nitrogen,

In raised beds you can easily apply fertilizer to only those plants that require supplemental feeding, like the zucchini in the right-hand bed.

but not as much as the salad greens. Fruits, such as cucumbers, melons, pumpkins, and squash, appreciate a supplement of phosphorus for good fruit-set development. Tomatoes, eggplants, and peppers also benefit from additional phosphorus, but their need is not as great. Vegetables with highly developed roots, such as garlic, leeks, onions, scallions, and shallots, require more potassium that the other macronutrients. The true root vegetables, such as beets, carrots, radishes, and turnips, also like some potassium supplementation. Beans and peas, which are able to fix nitrogen from the air into the soil, are considered soil builders as they do not deplete nutrients but rather benefit the soil they grow in.

Foliar Feeding

Until recently it was thought that the only way to feed a plant was through the soil — plants take up dissolved minerals and water through their roots. However, most plants can also take in nutrients through their leaves; they can be foliar fed. This practice does not work well with succulent plants, those with hairy leaves, or gray foliage plants. But the majority of fruits and vegetables can be given a boost by spraying food on their leaves. Fish emulsion and kelp are recommended for this type of feeding; many synthetic fertilizers may burn the leaves if applied directly.

As with any type of fertilizer, follow label instructions explicitly. Avoid foliar feeding in the heat of the day, in bright sun, or if the temperature is over 80° F. Heavy feeders, such as tomatoes, eggplants, and peppers, benefit from a foliar feeding every two weeks during the growing season.

WATER: THE ESSENCE OF LIFE

Without water, there is no life. Most plants are up to 90 percent water and, other than cacti and succulents, most plants cannot survive extended periods of drought. If you live in an area where water use is restricted, check with your local authorities to find out if there are any exceptions for edible gardens. In some localities, vegetable gardens are exempt from the surcharges imposed on watering lawns and ornamental plants.

Water is a valuable resource; make the most efficient use of it. The best way to water is to use drip irrigation. With this type of system, whether automated or manually controlled, water is released right at ground level, where the roots are; the amount of water lost to evaporation is minimal. Also, because the leaves don't get wet, the incidence of fungal diseases is decreased. You can buy kits (by mail order or in many garden centers and nurseries) and create your own customized system, complete with emitters, supply lines, and timers. The system can be as simple or as complicated as you wish.

Drip irrigation systems are especially suited for areas where the soil is not frequently turned or replanted. You may wish to use drip irrigation just around permanent plantings of herbs, tree and shrub fruit, and nuts in your kitchen garden. In cold winter areas (where the temperature remains below freezing for any length of time), drip irrigation systems must be drained and lifted for the winter. In

Railroad ties are excellent for creating raised beds. For edibles, do not use pressure-treated or creosoted lumber.

warm winter areas, you can leave the tubes down year-round. You may want to cover the lines with a layer of decorative mulch for aesthetics.

Another efficient method of watering is to use "leaky pipe" hoses. These hoses are made of recycled tires; water slowly seeps through them, delivering moisture right at ground level, near the root zone. It is fairly easy to snake these hoses through the garden. Using such a system you can water at any time of day or night, unlike using a sprinkler, which you only want to do during early daylight hours so that the leaves that get wet have a chance to dry off before nighttime.

Herbs as Companion Plants

The use of some plants as useful companions to others is long-standing. Although there have been no scientific studies either to validate or disprove companion planting, many gardeners devoutly pair certain herbs with vegetables.

Herb	Use
Basil	Protects squash and cucumbers from mildew
Borage	Protects cabbage from flea beetles
Chervil	Protects lettuce from aphids, mildew, snails, and slugs
Chives	Planted with roses to deter pests, blackspot, and mildew
Dill	Protects against carrot fly; discourages snails from lettuce
Fennel	Attracts bees that pollinate other plants
Garlic	Protects roses and lilies from mildew
Hyssop	Protects against cabbageworm, snails, and slugs
Lavender	Attracts bees that pollinate other plants
Sage	Protects against cabbageworm, aphids, snails, and slugs
Summer savory	Protects beans and peas from aphids
Thyme	Protects against cabbageworm, snails, and slugs

PESTS AND DISEASES

Although no garden is pest- and disease-proof, planting a diverse array of plants usually results in fewer problems. It is important to include a tree or shrub, preferably an evergreen, that will persist through the winter and provide a safe haven for praying mantises to deposit their egg cases. These insects eat a prodigious amount of aphids, whiteflies, and other garden pests.

By encouraging predators in the garden, you are discouraging the bad bugs. A delicate balance occurs: there are enough bad bugs to keep the predators happy, and this in turn keeps the bad guys under control. Some of the creatures you want to invite into your garden include snakes, birds, toads, and frogs. A clay pot turned on its side in a shady spot is a haven for a toad or frog. Feeding birds near the garden encourages them to come into the area.

If you find that you do have a pest or disease problem, before taking any steps to control it, make sure you correctly identify it. Your local Cooperative Extension Service can be of help. Many have telephone hotlines and offices where you can bring problem plants and pests for identification.

An Ounce of Prevention

To avoid an infestation, keep a keen eye on the garden. That means going out every day and, in addition to picking ripe fruits and vegetables, taking the time to look at the entire plant. Do the leaves look healthy? Are there holes in them? Do the fruits look succulent and juicy or are they wizened or misshapen? Are Japanese beetles having an orgy in the rugosa roses?

One of the best ways to deal with pests it to practice the tenets of IPM, Integrated Pest Management: 1. monitor the plants; 2. identify any pests; 3. assess the damage and decide whether or not you (and your plants) can live with that amount of damage; 4. if you have to treat the problem, use the least toxic method possible; 5. check for improvement or further damage.

You don't have to call out the bomb squad to deal with insect pests in the garden. Often a strong spray of water from the hose is enough to rid your plants of such pests as aphids and spider mites. Remember that most pesticides that you use in the garden, even organic ones like insecticidal soap, are not species specific; they will kill the good guys right along with the bad ones. Handpick insects early in the morning when they are slow to react. If only a small portion of a plant is diseased, cut it out and destroy that part; do not compost diseased plant material. To avoid spreading diseases, dip your pruners in alcohol after each cut you make.

Crop Rotation

Another way of preventing diseases in the kitchen garden is to practice crop rotation. This can be done on a three- or five-year cycle; no crop (or member of the same plant family) is planted in the same area for either three or five years. Thus, the various plant families are rotated through the garden. The one exception is the legume family; beans and peas are able to fix nitrogen from the air into the soil, helping to feed the soil as they grow, so they can be planted in any part of the garden at any time.

Plants and Their Families

Keeping each plant family in separate areas of the garden helps you keep track of crop rotation.

Curcubit	**Mustard**	**Nightshade**	**Beet**
cucumbers	broccoli	eggplants	beets
gourds	Brussels sprouts	peppers	spinach
melons	cabbage	potatoes	Swiss chard
pumpkins	cauliflower	tomatillos	
squashes	kales	tomatoes	
	kohlrabi		
	mustard		
	radishes		
	turnips		

Legume	**Onion**	**Carrot**
beans	garlic	carrots
peas	leeks	dill
soybeans	onions	fennel
scallions	parsley	
shallots	parsnips	

The versatility of the beds in Liz Ball's garden is demonstrated by the galvanized metal tubes sunk into the ground, which can either support trellises or serve as the base for plastic tubing that supports floating row cover above the strawberries. The row cover keeps the bed warmer in spring while keeping pests out.

CHAPTER 3
DESIGNING THE GARDEN

Design plays a major role in the kitchen garden. Certainly a potager is not just a mass of vegetables — it is put together in a pleasing manner, often following strict geometric designs. Yet don't let the concept of garden design scare you off. This chapter will show you some basic principles that will make creating a visually pleasing garden easy for anyone.

When planning and designing a flower bed or border, you take into account the height, shape, texture, and color of the various plants you're including. A kitchen garden should be thought out in the same manner. Plant the garden with the tallest plants in the back (or the middle if it is a bed that you view from all sides), and the shortest ones in the front or along the edge.

Many herbs are excellent edging plants, as are many greens. Although you tend to think of edging plants as low-growers, usually under 8 inches tall, the edgers can be taller depending on the types of plants in the beds. I always thought that marigolds were handsome paired with tomatoes, the yellow flowers setting off the vivid red of the fruit. Over the years, I've combined everything from sprawling, unstaked 'Red Currant' tomatoes, with their tiny, pea-sized fruit, and

The red cabbage leaves contrast well with the pale green 'Salad Bowl' lettuce leaves in the center bed in this kitchen garden, while in the border, the silvery Artemisia absinthium is a good foil for the purple-leafed amaranth.

Potted trees in the pathways as well as the white birches at the edge of the field provide a strong vertical element in this Long Island garden. In the middle of the center bed, a flowering onion will create a lovely lavender-topped exclamation point when it blooms.

'Yellow Gem' marigolds, with their attractive fernlike foliage, to the ribbed stuffing tomato 'Costoluto Genovese' and 36-inch-tall 'Inca' marigolds.

Depending on what else you grow in the potager, you can use plants that are anywhere from 6 to 24 inches tall to edge the garden. Some of the herbs and edible flowers are very lovely, such as basil (especially 'Spicy Globe', 'Purple Ruffles', and 'Dark Opal'), chives, dianthus, hyssop, lavender, marigolds, nasturtiums, oregano, pansies, parsley, rosemary (the creeping variety or a type that may be pruned), sage (look for purple, tricolor, golden sage, or large-leafed 'Berggarten' sages), sweet woodruff, thyme, tuberous begonias, tulips, and violets. I also like to use vegetables with attractive greens, such as beets, carrots, chicory, kohlrabi, lettuce, kale (especially ornamental varieties, which are as delicious as any other kale and extend the interest in the garden through late fall into winter), radishes, and the colorful heirloom varieties of Swiss chard. Heading plants, such as broccoli, cabbage, and cauliflower, also can be fun edgers for the garden.

HEIGHT

In the typical vegetable garden, height is the only consideration when placing plants. Obviously this holds true in any garden — you don't want the taller plants to shade out the shorter ones. Yet among the various heights of plants there are also different forms and textures that add interest to the garden. Corn, for instance, is tall and upright and can be used for a vertical accent. Fruit trees, even dwarf varieties, are also relatively tall but have a full, rounded habit. That is unless you grow the space-saving 'Colonnade' apple, which reaches about 8 feet tall with only a 2-foot spread from the trunk. This tree, with its unique columnar shape, can work equally well in a formal or informal garden.

Vertical Highlights

Tall plants provide vertical interest in the garden. They can be grouped together in the back of an edible border or used singly. In a garden that is viewed from all sides, use these plants singly (or with tall, narrow plants in groups of no more than three) for vertical punctuation. Some plants, such as yucca, send up a flower spike that is much taller than the rest of the plant.

Some of the more tropical plants, such as bananas and taro, are splendid vertical accents, with bold leaves that add another dimension to the garden. Although you don't think of asparagus as tall, their ferny summer foliage can grow 5 to 6 feet high. Artichokes and cardoon add a great vertical aspect combined with handsome silvery foliage. Some of the grains and flowering amaranths also bring excitement to the garden. Look to common vegetables and herbs like corn, lemon verbena, and fennel, or more uncommon ones like Jerusalem artichokes and orach for vertical interest. Some of the edible shrub blossoms, such as hibiscus, hollyhocks, pineapple guava, roses, and sunflowers, add color as well as height.

An espaliered pear tree is protected from the cold winds by training against the south-facing side of a shingled house.

Trees and Shrubs

Fruits and nuts, whether in tree or shrub form, are valuable additions to any kitchen garden. Generally, a tree is a single-stemmed woody plant that grows over 25 feet tall, while a shrub has multiple stems arising from the base and grows less than 25 feet tall. When including a tree or shrub in the garden, be sure its ultimate size is in proportion to the all-over scheme. For example, you would not want an American persimmon, which can reach over 30 feet tall, in a 10-foot-by-10-foot garden. If the tree you want is too large for the garden space, consider locating it in another area of your yard. As you look around your garden, think about replacing an overgrown shade tree with a fruit or nut tree. Either will provide equally good shade and will often have lovely blooms in spring with the added benefit of fruit or nuts in summer or fall. Just think of all the fruits and nuts you can grow, depending on your climate: almond, apple, apricot, avocado, banana, bay laurel, blackberry, blueberry, carambola (starfruit), cherimoya, cherry, chestnut, citrus (lemon, lime, orange, grapefruit, and many, many more), crabapple, currant, date, elderberry, fig, filbert, gooseberry, guava, hazelnut, hickory, jujube, kumquat, lilac, loquat, medlar, mulberry, natal plum, nectarine, olive, pawpaw, peach, pear, pecan, persimmon, pineapple guava, pistachio, plum, pomegranate, prickly pear, quince, raspberry, and walnut.

If space is a limiting factor and you want to grow fruit trees, consider training them as espaliers. Growing them flat against a wall or trellis creates a lovely edible backdrop to the garden. You can take the time over several years to train the trees yourself, or you can get trees that have already been in training for sev-

---

Trees and Shrubs for the Kitchen Garden

You can train these trees as espaliers or cordons for a more formal effect.

Almond	Crab apple	Plum
Apple	Medlar	Pomegranate
Apricot	Nectarine	Quince
Bay	Peach	
Citrus	Pear	

eral years. Many nurseries carry container-grown, espaliered dwarf apple and pear trees. I visited Alan Haskell's nursery in New Bedford, Massachusetts, last winter and was delighted to see the touch of whimsy in his own garden. He had attached artificial fruit to the large pear tree espaliered against his house — and, for the holidays, he had added an ornamental partridge.

For a unique border to the garden, create a Belgian fence by interweaving the branches of espaliered trees. It is especially attractive in the winter when the leaves are gone and you can appreciate the pattern of the branches.

Another space saver is dwarf trees. Some fruit trees are true genetic dwarf plants; others are the normal fruiting tree grafted onto dwarfing rootstock. Bear in mind that the designation "dwarf" is relative to the tree's usual size — a dwarf tree of one variety may be 15 feet tall, while another may be only 8 feet tall. There are even some dwarf trees that have a dwarfing rootstock plus a dwarf midstem, with the chosen variety grafted on top. You are more likely to find a good choice of dwarf trees in specialty nursery catalogs than in your local nursery or garden center.

Vines

Vining plants, with their unique growing habit, are quite versatile because their shape is determined by how they are trained. Although most vines can be allowed to sprawl and in that manner they can be grown as ground covers, it is preferable to give them vertical support. Training them upward allows for better air circulation around the plants, resulting in fewer disease and insect problems. It's also much easier to pick the edible portion of the plant when you don't have to stoop down to ground level. And the leaves or fruit that you're picking will be cleaner, with less soil splashed up onto them from rain or watering.

The support you use determines the effect these plants will have in the garden. Scarlet runner beans that are trained on a single stake will give the appearance of a narrow vertical column, while those trained on an arbor or trellis will provide a much more lush feeling. Pillars and obelisks made of wood or metal are handsome additions to gardens, even as ornaments without vining plants scrambling up them. Be creative with your supports — netting attached to fence posts works well to support cucumber vines, but they are much more interesting climbing up an old garden gate placed in the center of the plot.

Flower beds, edged with stones that came from the garden, soften the hard edges of the vegetable beds in Liz Ball's garden. The trellises install easily at the edges of the raised vegetable beds, providing support for peas in spring and tomatoes, beans, and cucumbers in summer.

Vines for Vertical Accent

These edibles are handsome in the garden trained on a support.

Asparagus bean	Grapes	Passion fruit
Canary creeper	Gourds	Peas
Chayote	Hops	Pole beans
Climbing nasturtiums	Hyacinth bean	Runner beans
Climbing roses	Kiwi	Tomatoes
Cucumber	Malabar spinach	

Sprawling heirloom roses are a fragrant backdrop for the formality of this four-square kitchen garden outside Richmond, Virginia. Unsprayed, they can also be enjoyed for their edible flowers.

When growing vines in the garden, take into account the ultimate height of the vine to determine the height of the support needed. Remember that a 6-foot tomato stake will not be long enough to support a tomato vine that grows 6 feet tall because at least 12 to 18 inches of the stake needs to be in the ground. Otherwise it is likely to topple as the tomato climbs to the top and the vine becomes heavy with fruit.

The contrasting textures of the leaves of (left to right) the potatoes, Brussels sprouts, and squash provide interest in a sea of green. The edible squash blossoms add vivid spots of color in this suburban New York garden.

FORM, SHAPE, AND TEXTURE

Form (or shape) and texture are given a lot of attention when you're putting together an ornamental garden but are often ignored in a kitchen garden. I feel they are as important, if not more important than color, however, because they provide a lot of the interest in gardens that are predominantly green foliage until the colorful flowers or fruit are in season.

Edibles with Interesting Form and/or Texture

When you start looking at edibles with an eye to design, it's amazing how much you notice.

Artichokes	large spiny leaves and handsome chokes that open to thistlelike flowers
Asparagus	fernlike foliage in summer
Basil	the ruffled leaves of 'Purple Ruffles'
Broccoli 'Romanesco'	whorled, pyramidal heads
Cabbages	round heads and the rippled, ruffled leaves of the Savoy types
Cardoon	large, bold, silvery foliage
Carrots	feathery foliage
Celery	upright dark green stems with a ruff of leaves (if not blanched)
Dill	feathery leaves
Endive, frisée types	finely cut curly leaves
Escarole	long curled leaves
Fennel	feathery leaves
Kale	oaklike leaves ('Lacinato' has narrow leaves, 'Scotch Curly' has finely cut curled leaves)
Kohlrabi	round heads on the ground with attractive leaves above
Leeks	fountainlike form
Lettuce, loose-leaf types	attractive leaves in many shapes: ruffled, oak-leaf, frilled, triangular
Mâche (Corn salad)	rosette of leaves
Onions	upright leaves
Parsley, curled	curled leaves
Prickly pear (Nopales)	cactus with flat round pads and spines
Radicchio	round heads
Rhubarb	large palmate leaves
Tomatoes	many shapes of fruit: small and round, pear-shaped, pleated, oval, large beefsteak type
Yucca	swordlike evergreen leaves

Eggplant 'Listada di Gandia'

VEGETABLES OF MANY COLORS

So many of the vegetables themselves are beautiful, and if you take the time to seek out some of the more unusual varieties (often you can find a wide range of color in heirloom vegetables), you'll be rewarded with rainbows of color in the garden. Tomatoes, for example, go far beyond the common red beefsteak type. In fact, when you see all the choices of tomatoes and other vegetables, you'll quickly realize that what we have come to know and eat is often the most uninteresting, both in looks and flavor.

Grow several different types of the same vegetable — not only do they make your garden look more interesting, but the genetic biodiversity lessens the chance of total crop failure. Site the plants in the garden so they show off their best attributes. 'Bright Lights' chard, with its yellow, orange, red, white, green, and

Colorful Vegetables for the Garden

You can find almost every color of the rainbow in a vegetable garden. For silver or grey, look to the silvery green foliage and chokes of artichokes and the long silvery green leaves of cardoon. 'Lemon' cucumber bears small, round, yellow fruit.

Purples and reds abound in the garden. 'Violetto' artichoke bears purple chokes. 'Royalty Purple Podded' bean has deep purple pods. 'Purple Sprouting' broccoli has deep purple-green heads. Grow 'Rubine' Brussels sprouts for its reddish purple stem and leaves. 'Lasso' and 'Ruby Perfection' cabbages have reddish purple heads. 'Violet Queen' and 'Purple Cape' cauliflowers have purple heads and they don't require blanching like most white cauliflowers. 'Ruby' ('Rhubarb') chard has gorgeous purple-red leaves and midribs. 'Purple Vienna' kohlrabi's purple heads are almost stately sitting on the ground. The red-leaf types of lettuce have a reddish to purplish tint to their leaves. Mustards can have majestic coloration: 'Osaka Purple' bears purple-red veined leaves, while 'Red Giant' leaves are burgundy-splotched. Red orach has purplish red leaves and stems. An unusual pea is 'Blue-Pod Capucijners', with bluish purple pods that follow bicolored (magenta-rose and lavender) edible flowers. The classic 'Giulio' radicchio has reddish purple leaves with white veins, while 'Rossa di Trevisio' has burgundy leaves variegated with white veins, but only after several frosts. Of course, there are the showy red stems of rhubarb that should be planted so they can be seen with the early morning or late afternoon sun illuminating them like shards of stained glass.

For hues of green, look to 'Romanesco' broccoli for its chartreuse heads. Try the various kales: 'Lacinato' has narrow, deep blue-green, rippled leaves, while 'Red Russian' has blue-green leaves with reddish-purple veining (its leaves turn reddish-purple after frost). 'Bleu du Solaise' leek has handsome blue-green leaves.

Multicolors can be found as well. 'Red Cranberry' beans have white pods tinged with cranberry. Beets bear green and red leaves. One of the most beautiful vegetables is Swiss chard — 'Bright Lights' has leaf midribs that are orange, yellow, red, pink, or silver. The more exotic varieties of eggplant come in a range of colors — yellow, orange, purple, white, bicolor lavender, and white.

Mature peppers range in color from pale yellow to deep red, chocolatey brown, purple, fiery orange, and golden yellow. 'Trifetti' pepper also has variegated leaves. Tomatoes range from near white to golden, red, orange, bicolored, purple, green, and striped.

gold stems, is especially lovely where the early morning or late afternoon sunlight can stream through the leaves, bringing them to life. Don't hide those gorgeous tomatoes, whether they're the handsome 'Purple Cherokee', the uniquely fuzzy 'Georgia Peach', the cherry gems of 'Sungold', or the tiny 'Red Currant' jewels. And how stunning orange Turkish eggplants are — and the original small white

'Bright Lights' chard is one of the most colorful vegetables, with ribs in hues of red, pink, yellow, orange, and white. Plant it where the rays of the rising or setting sun will illuminate the leaves; it looks like a living stained glass window. To extend its life in the garden, harvest individual outer leaves as needed; the plant will continue to put out new leaves.

The beauty of a kitchen garden extends to its bountiful harvest. You don't need a lot of space to grow a wide variety of produce.

eggplant that makes you understand how the plant got its name. As you lay out your kitchen garden, don't just think about the eventual harvest; think about the beauty of the plants as well and you'll be rewarded with a more attractive garden that you can appreciate any time of day.

Herbs of Different Colors

Most herbs have green leaves. For added interest, look for varieties with different colored foliage. Remember that many herbs add even more color to the garden when they bloom.

Herb	Variety	Color
Basil	'Dark Opal'	Deep purple leaves and stems
	'Holly's Painted'	Purple-splotched leaves
	'Purple Ruffles'	Dark purple leaves and stems
Bay	'Golden Bay'	Golden leaves
Fennel	'Bronze'	Brownish green leaves and stems (particularly lovely is the new growth, which looks like a ponytail)
Lemon balm, variegated		Gold-splashed leaves
Marjoram, golden		Gold-splashed to golden leaves
Mint, ginger		Gold-splashed leaves
Mint, orange bergamot		Purple- to bronze-tinged leaves
Mint, pineapple		Cream-edged leaves
Sage	'Icterina'	Yellow variegated leaves
	'Pupurascens'	Purple leaf
	'Tricolor'	Purple, deep pink, and white variegated leaves
Sorrel	'Red'	Red-veined leaves
Thyme, lemon	'Argenteus'	Silver-edged leaves
	'Aureus'	Gold-edged leaves

CHAPTER 4

FOR A BOUNTEOUS, VARIED HARVEST

Most books will tell you that vegetable gardens need to be in full sun, receiving a minimum of 6 hours of sun a day. That is true for most vegetables, but some will thrive in less light — 4 to 6 hours of sun a day. Many leafy greens, such as lettuce and kale, can survive the heat of summer if grown in cooler shade. I've planted both in the garden in early spring, when they get full sun. Then, as the days get longer and hotter, other plants around them, such as tomatoes and corn, grow up and effectively shade them from the heat.

Although they grow best with 8 hours of sun, you can still get a good harvest from these crops if they get 4 to 6 hours of sun a day: amaranth, beans, beets, borage, broccoli, Brussels sprouts, cabbage, calendula, cauliflower, celery, chard, chervil, cress, cucumber, endive, fava beans, kale, kohlrabi, lamb's quarters, leaf lettuces, leeks, miner's lettuce, nasturtiums, nettle, parsnip, peas, potato, pumpkin, purslane, radish, salsify, spinach, squash, rutabaga, and turnip.

You can also grow greens in the dappled shade of evergreen or deciduous trees, as well as the shade of buildings and fences. Only miner's lettuce, leaf let-

In late spring, you can see the amount of space allotted for the plants to reach maturity. Also, the geometric form of this Long Island kitchen garden is evident. Shrub roses are used for cut flowers and cooking.

tuce, and spinach will survive in deep shade. You'll notice that plants grown in less light have larger leaves to compensate for the lack of sun, and their fruits may not be as large as those from plants grown in full sun.

PRODUCTIVITY

Many gardeners, in an exuberance of planting, grow much more than their families can eat, and unless you plan to dry, freeze, or can the excess harvest, it's helpful to know how much you should grow. In winter the mail-order catalogs are so tempting, with their luscious color photographs and sumptuous descriptions of the myriad fruits and vegetables — I often order enough seed to plant my whole community! Because I am so hungry for the taste of a freshly picked tomato (or bean or pea — whatever it is I am reading about in the dead of winter when the garden harvest is long gone), I go overboard and order much more than I could possibly grow.

Consider ordering seed with several friends. Although you may plant every single sugar snap pea in a seed packet, it is unlikely that you want to grow out all fifteen tomato seeds. It is much more fun to grow several different kinds of tomatoes, for instance, in different colors and sizes, for all the uses you have for them in the kitchen — eating out of hand, salads, drying, cooking, sauces, etc.

Check out the Plant a Row for the Hungry program, sponsored by the Garden Writers Association of America. It is a simple, people-helping-people program whereby you simply grow a row (or several plants) more than you normally would in the garden and donate the harvest to your local food bank, shelter, or soup kitchen. They are always happy to get fresh produce in season. For more information about where fresh food is needed in your community, call Second Harvest (312) 263-2303.

If you don't use all the seed from a packet, you can store whatever's left over in an envelope in a cool, dry place until planting time next season or next year. Most vegetable seeds remain viable for a number of years. Several years ago I didn't buy any new seed; I just used seed from all the leftover packets I'd been saving for the past ten years. Even though the germination rate goes down the longer the seed is stored, I still had more than enough seedlings to fill my garden and share with my local horticultural society.

Nasturtiums are among the most commonly grown edible flowers, prized for their peppery blooms and leaves. Their vivid colors — red, yellow, and orange — add a bold note to any kitchen garden.

If you have any doubt about whether or not seeds are still good, you can do a simple germination test. Moisten a paper towel and place five seeds on it. Roll the towel up and place it in a plastic bag away from direct sunlight. Check the seeds daily to see if they've sprouted. Newly purchased seeds should have a germination rate of at least 90 percent (check the seed packet for specific information on each variety). However, you may be satisfied with a germination rate of 50 percent or less for old seeds of some vegetables like squash. Even if only a couple germinate, that can be enough for a garden. See Appendix 1, page 112, for viability of seeds.

How Much Is Enough?

Many gardeners know what vegetables they want to grow but are uncertain how many plants they really need to keep them in fresh produce throughout the growing season. Many books offer up charts of how many plants or rows of a particular plant are needed to feed a family of four, for example. These figures may be misleading, depending on whether you are looking to eat only fresh from the garden or whether you plan on canning or freezing some of the harvest for out-of-season use. The chart in the appendix (page 112) offers the yield per 10 feet of row; then you can decide how much you want to harvest and figure out how many feet to plant.

Is It Ready Yet?

A good gardener is like a good cook who can coordinate a five-course meal and have all of the dishes in each course ready at the right time. Most of us don't have the luxury of unlimited space, so we overlap crops in the garden. You need to have an idea of what grows when and how long it takes to mature. For example, you can start cucumbers growing in the same place that peas grew in the cool of spring; by the time it is warm enough to put cucumbers in the ground, the pea harvest is nearly over. Plant the cucumbers 6 to 8 inches away from the trellis and as they start to wind their way upwards, you will have had the final harvest from the peas (if Mother Nature is cooperative).

In small gardens, it's best to use transplants rather than sowing seed directly in the garden. If you start the seeds indoors yourself, you have a bit more control of the germination rate and time — you can provide bottom heat for those

Bush cucumbers will bear fruit about two months after transplanting into the garden (see box on page 56).

plants that require warm soil, regardless of whether it is cold and damp outside, where the seeds would likely rot. Then when the weather is nice and warm (or cool, depending on the plant), you can pop the hardened-off transplants right into the garden. Using transplants (whether those you've grown from seed or purchased at a nursery or garden center) also saves time — you don't have to thin the plantings as you would have to if you grew directly from seed in the garden.

Most beginning gardeners just go to the local nursery or garden center and buy small plants. The plants are often in cell packs of four or six plants or in small individual pots. When shopping, it's important to buy only strong, healthy plants. Don't consider any that have pale or mottled leaves — this could be a sign of disease or that they've been in a small pot too long. Lift up the pot or cell pack. If roots are growing out of the bottom, don't buy that plant. Look on the under-

A plastic-covered frame greenhouse gives this northern kitchen garden a jump-start on the growing season, providing a place for starting plants so they are ready to move out into the garden as soon as the weather warms.

side of leaves for any signs of marauding insects — whitefly, aphids, or others. You don't want plants that are already flowering or fruiting; they won't give you a good harvest because they are already too mature. Avoid plants that are wilted.

Once you get the plants home, put them in the shade and get them into the garden as soon as you can. It's always best to transplant in late afternoon or on a cloudy day; this stresses the plant less. Make sure to keep transplants well watered — you may have to water them every day until they are established in the garden.

To Seed or Not to Seed

Once you've decided what you want to grow, you have to decide whether you are planting seed directly in the garden or starting the seeds indoors and putting transplants into the garden beds. Having lived most of my life in areas with cold winters and relatively long, cool springs, I've preferred to put small plants into the garden whenever possible. The main advantage is that I get a head start on the growing season. Many seeds just won't germinate until the soil has warmed. In fact, some seeds, such as corn and lima beans, will just rot if the soil is too cool and damp. I begin to grow plants indoors about three months before the

Best Planting Methods for Garden Vegetables

The vegetables noted with an asterisk are worth trying to grow by the method listed, although it may not be the usually recommended method. Direct seeding works well for the asterisk-marked vegetables in mild winter areas.

Transplants	Direct Seed
Basil	* Basil
* Beans	Beans
* Beets (transplant when very young)	Beets
Broccoli	* Broccoli
Brussels sprouts	* Cabbages
Cabbages	Carrots
Cauliflower	* Cauliflower
* Corn	Corn
Eggplants	Kohlrabi
Leeks	Leeks
Lettuces	Melons
* Melons	Onions
Onions	Peas
Peppers	Pumpkins
Perennial herbs	Radishes
Pumpkins	Scallions
Squashes	Spinach
Tomatoes	Squashes

last frost date and keep starting new ones well into the growing season. That also allows me to have seedlings to interplant with early and late crops, making for optimum use of the garden. I even start broccoli, kale, and other cool weather vegetables indoors in July to plant out in the garden in August; it's much cooler indoors at that time of year than outside.

Since I don't plant in rows but rather in groups, it's much easier to keep track of what's in the garden when I plant seedlings, rather than waiting for seeds to come up. Direct planting also eliminates the need for thinning. Some plants, however, just don't grow well from transplants, especially those with fleshy roots, like carrots or beets. Others grow so quickly, there's little benefit to starting them indoors. Dill and fennel also don't transplant well, if you are cultivating them for their leaves. The stress of transplanting triggers them to bloom early; this is not a problem if you enjoy their edible flowers.

When starting seeds indoors, I've found it best to make two sowings of the same seed, a week to two apart. That way, if the weather is unseasonably cool, the plants that you started at the proper (ideal) time may get too big before the conditions are right to plant. Those started a week or two later 'are a good fall-back. If your timing and the weather are perfect, you have several choices — you can give away the extra plants, participate in the Plant a Row for the Hungry program (see page 48), or encourage a neighborhood child to garden and share plants and garden with him or her.

It seems so simple — plant a seed and in time it will grow into a plant, which in turn you can harvest. Some seeds prefer to germinate in cool temperatures, while others prefer it warmer. If you are sowing a lot of your seed directly into the garden, a soil thermometer is a good investment. You can also use the thermometer indoors to monitor the temperature of the soil in the flats or pots in which you're starting seeds. This is especially important if you are using heating cable to warm the soil; you don't want it to get too hot.

Every beginning gardener plants his or her first seed and then expects it to sprout overnight. Patience can be a virtue, but how long do you wait for the seedling to emerge before you begin to worry that something has gone wrong? The chart in the appendix (page 113) gives you the range of temperatures and times it takes to get seeds started, as well as the temperature they prefer (nighttime low to daytime high) once they're up and growing.

Fall Is for Bountiful Harvests

The garden industry has done a good job in the past few years of educating people about fall planting. We've all seen or heard the slogan, "Fall is for planting." Fall is also a great time in the kitchen garden, with harvests that outdo those of summer.

So many gardeners are so concerned with getting crops planted in the spring that they neglect summer planting for fall harvest. Many of the cool weather crops, such as the brassicas — mustard, broccoli, cauliflower, cabbage, and kale — actually perform better in the garden when the days get progressively cooler — no chance of bolting in October like there is in June.

In order to plan for a fall harvest, in the cold winter areas you have to work backwards. The point of reference is the first frost date in autumn. You can easily find out that date by contacting your local cooperative extension service.

'Stonehead' cabbage, usually grown in spring, also makes an excellent fall crop in most areas.

Then, using the chart below, calculate the planting date by subtracting the number of weeks from the first frost date. Of course, you need to plan the spring and summer garden so that you will have space to replant in July. As with a spring garden, for an extended harvest, stagger plantings over several weeks.

Pollination Produces Fruit

Many of the plants we call vegetables are actually fruits; that is, the flower was fertilized and the ovary swelled, producing a fleshy fruit that surrounds the seeds.

Days to Maturity (from transplant)

When you start your own seeds, you have the advantage of having the information on the seed packet. If you are buying transplants from a nursery or garden center, it helps to have this information when planning the garden for the entire season. This way you'll know which plants can follow others in succession, in order to keep the garden as productive as possible.

Less than 60 days	60 to 90 days	More than 90 days
Lettuces	Beets	Beets
Kohlrabi	Broccoli	Brussels sprouts
Radishes	Bush beans	Carrots
Salad greens	Cabbages	Corn
Spinach	Carrots	Eggplants
	Cauliflower	Garlic
	Corn	Melons
	Cucumbers	Onions
	Endive	Parsley
	Lettuces	Parsnips
	Peas	Peppers
	Potatoes	Pole beans
	Scallions	Potatoes
		Pumpkins
		Shallots
		Squashes
		Tomatoes

Flowering Plants to Attract Pollinators

Include some of these flowering trees and perennials in your garden to attract bees and other pollinators to nearby plants.

Common Name	Botanic Name
Aster	*Aster* spp.
Clover	*Trifolium* spp.
Fireweed	*Epilobium angustifolium*
Goldenrod	*Solidago* spp.
Gooseneck loosestrife	*Lysimachia clethroides*
Highbush blueberry	*Vaccinium corymbosum*
Hollyhock	*Alcea rosea*
Lemon balm	*Melissa officinalis*
Linden	*Tilia* spp.
Locust	*Robinia* spp.
Milkweed	*Aesclepias tuberosa*
Pincushion flower	*Scabiosa* spp.
Sea holly	*Eryngium* spp.
Sumac	*Rhus* spp.
Vetch	*Vicia* spp.

These "vegetables" include tomatoes, eggplants, peppers, squashes, pumpkins, tomatillos, and others. In order for pollination to take place, and ultimately for fruit to set, the pollen (usually from one plant or flower) has to get transferred from one flower to another. Although some pollen is wind-borne, most plants require an insect (most often honeybees) to do the pollinating. It can be helpful to have some plants that are sure to attract these pollinators to the garden; while they are busy working their favorite plants, they'll likely pollinate others as well.

REAPING THE REWARDS

The true joy of a kitchen garden begins when you eat the first spring greens in a salad, taste the sweet lushness of a sun-warmed ripe tomato, or savor the crispness of an apple right off the tree. For optimum enjoyment, pick fruit and veg-

The flowers of 'Scarlet Runner' beans have a delicious, beany flavor; they are a colorful and flavorful addition to a summer potato salad.

Seasonal Preferences

Vegetables will do best when grown in their preferred seasons.

Spring (Cool)	Summer (Hot)	Fall (Cool)
Beets	Beans	Beets
Broccoli	Corn	Broccoli
Brussels sprouts	Cucumbers	Cabbages
Cabbages	Eggplants	Carrots
Carrots	Melons	Endive
Cauliflower	Peppers	Kohlrabi
Kohlrabi	Pumpkins	Lettuces
Lettuces	Squashes	Radishes
Onions	Tomatoes	Spinach
Parsnips		Turnips
Peas		
Radishes		
Scallions		
Spinach		
Turnips		

etables from your garden at the peak of ripeness to eat that day. Don't spoil the flavor of tomatoes by picking them when they are unripe and then storing them in the refrigerator. Using your harvest promptly also assures maximum nutritional benefits. The potency level of many vitamins decreases proportionally from the time the vegetable is picked. Week-old spinach, for example, has lost as many nutrients as cooked, canned spinach. Here are some tips for harvesting the fruits and vegetables from your garden.

Asparagus — In spring, cut the spears at soil level when they are 6 to 8 inches tall and before the tips start to open.

Beets — Pick some of the greens (use as a spinach substitute, raw or cooked) when the leaves are 4 to 6 inches long. Harvest the tops and roots as "baby beets" when they are less than $1\frac{1}{2}$ inches in diameter. Or, wait until the roots are $1\frac{1}{2}$ to 3 inches in diameter for sweet beets.

Broccoli — Cut the main head when it is fully developed and before individual flowers begin to open. With a sharp knife, cut 6 to 7 inches below the head. Allow sideshoots to develop.

Cabbage — Cut the head when it is of mature size, solid and firm.

Cantaloupe — Hold the melon in one hand and push against the attached stem with the other thumb. When ripe, the stem slips off with only slight pressure. However, in areas with a lot of rain during harvest season, it's best to pick the melons before they are completely ripe; otherwise, the excess moisture will ruin the flavor by cutting down on the sugar content.

Carrots — Harvest when 3/4 inch to 2 inches in diameter. If the weather remains cool and dry in the fall, leave the carrots in the ground and harvest later.

Cauliflower — Cut the head when it is of mature size and the curds are firm and still white. With a sharp knife, cut several inches below the head. Allow sideshoots to develop.

Celery — Harvest when the plants are 12 to 15 inches tall. Young tender stems may be cut individually when they are 6 to 10 inches long.

Collards — Harvest when the inner leaves are 6 to 8 inches long.

Corn — Pick when the silk is dry and brown; the kernels should pop when pressed with your thumbnail and thick milky liquid should emerge.

Cucumber — Pick when fruit is almost mature size (6 to 9 inches long) and the skin is still bright green and firm.

Eggplant — Harvest when fruits are 4 to 6 inches in diameter, firm and bright in color, not dull.

Garlic — Pull when foliage turns brown and tops start to fall over.

Kale — Cut when outer leaves are 8 to 10 inches long; harvest individual leaves. Plant will continue to produce new leaves. Harvest newer leaves when 6 to 8 inches long.

Kohlrabi — Harvest when the "ball" above the ground is 2 to 3 inches in diameter.

Lettuce — Leaf types: harvest outer leaves when 4 to 6 inches long; inner leaves will continue to grow. Romaine lettuce: harvest entire plant at base when it is 8 to 12 inches tall. Bibb lettuce: cut entire plant when it is 4 inches in diameter.

Fordhook lima beans are an old favorite with good flavor, whether they are picked when small or mature.

Lima beans — Pick when the beans and pods are full size, but before they begin to dry out. Only the seeds (beans) of limas are edible, not the pods.

Mustard greens — Cut when outer leaves are 6 to 8 inches long. Cut outer leaves, then continue to harvest inner ones.

Okra — Pick when pods are about 6 inches long. Wear long sleeves and gloves to protect your skin.

Onions — Pull when most of the tops have fallen over. After pulling them out of ground, wash onions and leave them in shade for several days to cure.

Parsnips — Pull in late fall, after frost. Mulch thickly and they can be harvested all winter, until very early spring, before new growth starts.

Peas — Pick when the pods are fully developed and bright green. Peas with edible pods: harvest when they're about 3 inches long, before seeds enlarge.

Peppers — Pick when the fruits are firm and of mature color — red, yellow, orange, purple. This mature flavor is far superior to the unripe green.

Pinto beans — Harvest immature pintos as snap beans. When they are almost mature (full-size, but before they begin to dry out), pick them and use them like shelling beans, or leave them on the vine to mature completely and harvest them as dry beans.

Potatoes — Dig when the tubers are full-size and skin is firm. You can harvest "new" potatoes when they are about $1\frac{1}{2}$ inches in diameter.

Pumpkins — Harvest when the fruit has reached mature size, the skin is firm and slightly shiny, and the bottom is cream to orange in color.

Radishes — Pull when the roots are 1 to $1\frac{1}{2}$ inches in diameter.

Snap beans — Pick when the pod, when bent double, does not snap in two; otherwise they are either immature or too mature.

Spinach — Harvest when the outer leaves are 4 to 6 inches long; inner leaves will continue to develop.

'Little Bear' pumpkin, with its diminutive fruit, is a favorite in children's gardens.

Harvest 'Pattypan' squash when it is 1 to 2 inches across and use it as a "baby" vegetable — excellent raw or stir-fried.

Squash — Zucchini and yellow squash: pick when fruits are small, before they reach full size. Check them every other day to avoid the overnight-baseball-bat syndrome common with zucchini. Winter squash: pick when full-size (according to the seed packet), before frost.

Swiss chard — Pick when the leaves are 6 to 8 inches long.

Tomatoes — Harvest when fruit is the mature color (red, orange, yellow) and fairly uniform. Read the description of the variety, however. Some, like 'Purple Cherokee', have green shoulders (the upper portion of the tomato) even when ripe. The fruit should come off the stem easily without pulling.

Turnips — Harvest when the roots are 2 to $2\frac{1}{2}$ inches across, before a heavy frost. Harvest the leaves (greens) when 6 to 8 inches long.

Watermelon — Pick when it is the right size (according to the seed packet) for maturity. When you thump it with your knuckles, it should make a low *thud* sound; when unripe, it is higher pitched. Also, the tendril at the stem end of the melon turns brown, and the color of the bottom of the melon (touching the ground) changes from green to white or cream color.

Too Much of a Good Thing

Some people plant their kitchen gardens for fresh produce throughout the growing season, while others grow enough so that they can preserve some of the harvest for out-of-season use. I've found that even though I think I've planned my garden primarily for fresh harvest, there comes the day when there are more tomatoes and basil, for example, than I can possibly use. Then I have to decide which is the best storage method for them, depending on how soon I plan to use them. If I plan to use the basil within a couple of days, I cut them stems and place them in a glass of water on my kitchen counter; refrigerating them will cause the leaves to blacken. I recut the stems and change the water daily. Often I'll make a big batch of pesto with the basil and freeze it in portion sizes. Or I'll puree the basil with a bit of water and freeze it in ice cube trays. Once they're frozen, I put all the ice cubes in a resealable plastic freezer bag; then in winter, when I want to add the flavor of fresh basil to a soup, stew, or sauce, I can simply drop in a basil cube. Basil leaves don't freeze well when whole — they turn black — but their flavor is all right. You can also hang stems of basil upside down in a cool, dry place to let the leaves dry. Once they're dry, pick them off the stem and store in an airtight container.

If possible, never refrigerate tomatoes as their flavor diminishes with the cold. If you must chill them, let them warm up to room temperature before serving them. If I have an abundance of little cherry tomatoes or small paste-type 'Roma' tomatoes, I'll wash them off, slice them, and dry them in a dehydrator. If you live in a dry climate, you can air dry tomatoes (as well as other fruits and vegetables) on mesh or screen in a shady, well-ventilated area. On Long Island, where I lived for most of my gardening life, and Des Moines, where I now live, the summers are too humid to air-dry produce successfully. When I've tried, the tomatoes have rotted rather than dried. If you don't have a dehydrator, you can dry sliced vegetables and fruits in the oven, set at the lowest possible setting. Drying may take a few hours to a few days, depending on the thickness and water content of the fruit or vegetable and the relative humidity. I peel and chop larger tomatoes (discarding much of the seeds and liquid) and freeze them in one-cup, one-pint, and one-quart containers to use later on. They can be added to vegetable dishes or made into a fresh tomato sauce — a refreshingly summery taste with hot pasta on a cold winter's day.

A harvest of edible flowers includes calendulas, pansies, Johnny-jump-ups, chives, broccoli, scented geraniums, borage, nasturtiums, daylilies, society garlic, and lemons.

Edible Flowers

Common Name	Botanic Name	Flavor
Anise hyssop	*Agastache foeniculum*	Licorice
Apple	*Malus* spp.	Floral
Arugula	*Eruca vesicaria sativa*	Peppery
Basil	*Ocimum basilicum*	Herbal
Bee balm	*Monarda didyma*	Spicy/sweet
Borage	*Borago officinalis*	Cucumber
Broccoli	*Brassica oleracea*, Botrytis group	Spicy
Calendula	*Calendula officinalis*	Slightly bitter
Chamomile	*Anthemis nobilis*	Apple
Chicory	*Cichorium intybus*	Slightly bitter
Chives	*Allium schoenoprasum*	Oniony
Chrysanthemum	*Dendranthema × grandiflorum*	Mild to slightly bitter
Coriander (Cilantro)	*Coriandrum sativum*	Herbal
Dandelion	*Taraxacum officinale*	Sweet to slightly bitter
Daylily	*Hemerocallis* spp.	Sweet to vegetal
Dianthus	*Dianthus caryophyllus*	Sweet, clovey
Dill	*Anethum graveolens*	Herbal
Elderberry	*Sambucus canadensis*	Sweet
English daisy	*Bellis perennis*	Slightly bitter
Fennel	*Foeniculum vulgare*	Herbal
Garlic chives	*Allium tuberosum*	Garlicky
Hibiscus	*Hibiscus rosa-sinensis*	Mild citrus
Hollyhock	*Alcea rosea*	Mild nutty
Honeysuckle	*Lonicera japonica*	Sweet floral
Hyssop	*Hyssopus officinalis*	Strong herbal
Jasmine	*Jasminum sambac* and *J. officinale*	Sweet floral
Johnny-jump-up	*Viola tricolor*	Slightly minty
Kale	*Brassica oleracea*, Acephala group	Spicy
Lavender	*Lavandula* spp.	Strong floral
Lemon	*Citrus limon*	Sweet citrus
Lemon verbena	*Aloysia triphylla*	Sweet citrus
Lilac	*Syringa* spp.	Floral
Linden	*Tilia* spp.	Sweet
Marjoram	*Origanum vulgare*	Herbal

Common Name	Botanic Name	Flavor
Mint	*Mentha* spp.	Minty
Mustard	*Brassica juncea*	Spicy
Nasturtiums	*Tropaeolum majus*	Peppery
Nodding onion	*Allium cernuum*	Oniony
Okra	*Abelmoschus aesculentus*	Mild, sweet
Orange	*Citrus sinensis*	Sweet citrus
Oregano	*Origanum* spp.	Herbal
Pansy	*Viola × wittrockiana*	Slightly minty
Pea	*Pisum sativum*	Pealike
Pineapple guava	*Feijoa sellowiana*	Sweet tropical
Pineapple sage	*Salvia elegans*	Spicy sweet
Radish	*Raphanus sativus*	Peppery
Red clover	*Trifolium pratense*	Sweet
Redbud	*Cercis canadensis*	Pealike
Rose	*Rosa* spp.	Floral
Rose of Sharon	*Hibiscus syriacus*	Mild
Roselle	*Hibiscus sabdariffa*	Mild citrus
Rosemary	*Rosmarinus officinalis*	Herbal
Runner bean	*Phaseolus coccineus*	Beanlike
Safflower	*Carthamus tinctorius*	Bitter
Sage	*Salvia officinalis*	Herbal
Scented geranium	*Pelargonium* spp.	Floral
Signet marigold	*Tagetes tenuifolia*	Citrusy tarragon
Shungiku	*Chrysanthemum coronarium*	Slightly bitter
Society garlic	*Tulbaghia violacea*	Sweet garlicky
Squash blossoms	*Cucurbita pepo* spp.	Vegetal
Summer savory	*Satureja hortensis*	Herbal
Sunflower	*Helianthus annuus*	Bittersweet
Sweet woodruff	*Galium odoratum*	Fresh, sweet
Thyme	*Thymus* spp.	Herbal
Tuberous begonia	*Begonia × tuberhybrida*	Citrus
Tulip	*Tulipa* spp.	Bean- or pealike
Violet	*Viola odorata*	Sweet floral
Winter savory	*Satureja montana*	Herbal
Yucca	*Yucca* spp.	Sweet

Getting the Most Out of the Plants in Your Garden

From my standpoint, always having gardened in a relatively small space, I like to use plants in my kitchen garden that serve at least two functions — beauty and edibility. Perhaps this is the appeal of edible flowers for me — the same plants that are so gorgeous are incredibly tasty, too. Not all flowers are edible; indeed there are a number of poisonous flowers, so it is important to know exactly what you're eating. For that reason, I am including the botanic as well as the common name (which can differ from region to region) on the list of edible flowers.

I also like to showcase edibles with attractive flowers, even though the edible portion of the plant may be the leaves or fruit, such as eggplant (with lovely pale purple, inedible flowers).

Come Again, Please

I am basically a lazy gardener; it's just that there are only so many hours in a day and there are many things I would rather do in that time than weed or water. Good planning and mulching techniques help to cut down on those chores.

I honestly enjoy planning and harvesting the garden more than actually planting it, so in my gardens, the plants that grow all by themselves, with no help from me, are encouraged. Below is a selection of plants that will self-seed or self-sow in the garden.

Self-Sowing Plants

When allowed to flower and set seed, these plants will happily resow themselves in the garden. Those marked with an asterisk are more well-mannered than the others, generally dropping their seeds close to the mother plant.

Chervil	Johnny-jump-ups	Orach
Cilantro (Coriander)	* Lettuce	Oregano
Fennel	Love-in-a-mist	Perilla
Feverfew	Marigolds	Violets
* Hollyhocks	Mustard	

As Oscar Wilde, a man of great wit and wisdom, said, "For every gain there is a loss and every loss there is a gain." Self-sown plants are a mixed blessing; they have no regard for the design of a garden. They come up anywhere, and often, it seems, everywhere except where you actually want them. The first year I grew bronze fennel, I became enamored of the plant, with its deeply colored, feathery foliage. It did not bloom the first year, and the winter was very mild. The second spring, I was thrilled when it came back in the same place. The new growth looked like shiny auburn ponytails. The plant flowered magnificently in the summer, and I enjoyed cooking with the anise-flavored blooms. I didn't harvest all of the flowers and many went to seed — a fact about which I was not truly cognizant until the third spring. That year, not only did my original plant come back, more vigorous than ever, but dozens of baby plants popped up all over the garden and even in the lawn. I spent hours pulling out the fennel seedlings that spring as they kept appearing among other plants, yet leaving some that made serendipitous pairings with other plants like sage and Johnny-jump-ups.

At the other end of the self-sowing scale, Johnny-jump-ups, with their cute purple, yellow, and white faces, are a joy to me wherever they come up. The plants themselves are much more delicate than fennel as they grow, and with their diminutive stature they can easily cavort with any other plant.

Most of the self-sowers are annuals — plants that germinate, make leaves, flower, set seed, and die all within one growing season. Hollyhocks, however, are biennials — plants that put out a rosette of leaves the first year and don't flower until the second year. Many gardeners assume that they are perennials, as they seem to bloom in the same space year after year (although often the colors are not the same). Hollyhock seeds that drop to the ground in summer germinate and set out leaves before the first frost. The next spring is actually the seedlings' second year, and they bloom.

It's up to you whether you want to encourage or discourage self-sowing plants' prolific nature. It is quite easy to discourage them by cutting off the flowers before they have a chance to set seed and ripen. They need little or no encouragement to keep from proliferating in your garden — just be sure not to mulch too early in the season or you'll smother the seeds that might otherwise germinate. Also, learn what the seedlings look like so you don't inadvertently weed them out.

Certain aspects of this kitchen garden turn it into an evening garden, especially the night-fragrant, white-flowered Nicotiana sylvestris *(flowering tobacco) and the silver-leafed* Artemisia absinthium.

The Kitchen Garden at Night

Evening gardens are becoming popular, especially among all of us who work all day long and have little time to really enjoy the garden. Included in these gardens are plants that are visible in the waning light of dusk and the darkness that follows. With a little creativity, a kitchen garden can easily serve as an evening garden as well.

Several gourds (including one with edible young shoots) have fragrant white flowers that bloom at night. White eggplants show up well in the evening, especially if the plants are located near the edge of the garden. Look to variegated plants as well for nighttime interest — the lighter portion of the variegation shows up in the dimmest light.

Some vegetables, like radicchio, are naturally variegated with white veins or ribs. Other variegations are rarer, but you can find variegated corn, bananas, and even lemons in specialty catalogs. Many herbs have variegated forms that are readily found in nurseries and garden centers, including thyme (silver- and gold-edged), sage (golden and tricolor), and mint (variegated apple and ginger mints). 'Alaska' nasturtium is a particular favorite, with its variegated edible leaves and peppery-flavored orange blossoms.

Silver-leaved plants, such as lavender and artichoke, show up well in the evening, reflecting any available light. On all but moonless nights you can pick them out, even in an unlighted garden. These plants are also fairly drought tolerant — a boon for gardeners in dry climates.

Although a complete evening garden may not be in your plans, include a few of these plants to make your garden more interesting for the times you are in your garden or looking at your garden after sunset.

CHAPTER 5
THE KITCHEN GARDENS

Kitchen gardens are as unique as their creators. Here is a representative sampling of kitchen gardens from around the country. They range in size from about 10 square feet (Boxed Salad Garden) to almost an acre (Heliotrope Garden) and from informal to very formal designs. Within these pages you can find inspiration for your own garden, wherever you live. Follow these gardeners' examples and substitute some of your favorite edibles for some included in these plant lists.

In my edible flower garden, I trained garden peas up a small wooden trellis whose color blended into the brick wall. Peas were fronted by chamomile and 'Antique Shades' pansies.

KATE KERIVAN'S BOXED SALAD GARDEN
NEW HAMPSHIRE
(Hardiness Zone 4)

This compact garden comprises two raised, boxed-in beds. In a cold climate like this, getting a jump on the growing season in spring is important. The raised beds warm up quicker and dry out faster after the spring thaw than the surrounding ground, extending the growing season by several weeks to a month. Each bed is approximately 10 square feet.

These beds are used almost exclusively for growing salad greens, with the addition of a few herbs (also good in salads) and edible flowers. Harvest begins early, when the plants are thinned in spring, and continues right through the summer into fall. In late summer there is a second planting of lettuce, kale, and chard. The lettuce and chard are harvested until the first frost — the kale lasts well into the winter, especially if protected with a salt hay mulch. (Note: In my own Long Island garden, Zone 7, spring-planted kale will thrive all year if the summer is not too hot. Fall-planted kale is as beautiful in the garden in winter as it is delicious. I simply harvest a few outer leaves as I need them, and the plant keeps producing new ones. The following spring, the plant blooms and is a beautiful sight; the flowers have a slight sharpness to them and are attractive on a salad of mixed garden greens.)

The use of color and texture is important in this garden, especially in the varying hues and shades of green (parsley, amaranth, calendula leaves, kale) and red (chard, amaranth, fennel, mustard, kale, lettuce). The marigold and calendula flowers are both bright yellow punctuation marks, as are the kale blossoms if the plants are allowed to overwinter. In late spring, the sage sends up spikes of gorgeous, purplish blue edible flowers.

Boxed Salad Garden Plant List

Amaranth
Calendula
Chard 'Ruby'
Bronze fennel
Kale: 'Red Russian' and 'Scotch Lassie'
Lettuce: 'Juliet', 'Red Sails' and
    'Rouge d'Hiver'
Marigold 'Lemon Gem'
Mustard 'Japanese Red'
Parsley: curly and Italian flat-leaf
Sage

In the boxed garden, interest comes from the variations in shades of green as well as from the texture of leaves such as calendula, marigold 'Lemon Gem', 'Ruby' chard, 'Red Russian' and 'Scotch Lassie' kale, and several varieties of lettuce, including 'Juliet', 'Red Sails', and 'Rouge d'Hiver'.

POTAGER, MADOO CONSERVANCY
SAGAPONACK, NEW YORK
(Hardiness Zone 6)

Artist Robert Dash's property became the Madoo Conservancy in 1991. Although it is only two acres, it seems much larger because the paths wind you through eleven separate gardens. The potager lies between the summer studio/house and Barnsley's (a Norfolk terrier) kennel. Never did a dog have such a lovely view from inside his quarters. At one end of the garden the bold foliage of cardoon and hollyhocks provide privacy for the bathroom window, although the view of the garden from the bathroom is perfect.

The potager is designed in a traditional style. Many of the beds are edged with dwarf 'Vardar's Valley' boxwood, pruned into 1-foot-tall ball shapes; other beds are whimsically edged with 'Spicy Globe' basil, which naturally grows in the same shape as the boxwood and has similar size leaves. At the very center of the garden is a double arch, painted lilac (one of Dash's signature colors in the garden hardscape), up which a magnificent clematis wends its way skyward.

The display in the potager is always changing; Dash is as likely to select plants for their architectural form or color as for their use in the kitchen. He does grow what he likes to cook, favoring vegetables for salads and pesto. Lettuces not eaten are allowed to bolt and are enjoyed for their beauty. Inverted Portuguese terra cotta water pots are put out for the birds.

Always the artist, Dash creates a tableau: several watering cans and flower jugs are just outside the gate, as though a gardener were about to come out to retrieve them. Similarly, a hat appears to have been tossed on the

Madoo Conservancy Plant List

Basil: 'Spicy Globe' and 'Genovese'
Boxwood 'Vardar's Valley'
Cabbage
Cardoon
Celeriac
Chives
Clematis
Egyptian onions
Fennel
Hollyhocks
Lettuce
Lilies
Malabar spinach
Nasturtiums
Onions
Parsley
Peppers
Pole beans
Squash
Thyme
Welsh onions

The Madoo Potager has a double arch with vining clematis as a focal point. 'Spicy Globe' basil, with its rounded form, mimics the clipped boxwood.

Although Dash never cuts flowers from the garden to bring inside, the pitcher near the gate looks ready to receive freshly cut flowers.

garden gate, and several heads of garlic lay as if they have just been pulled out of the earth. Dash uses bright colors in the hardscape in small amounts. The finial of the garden gate is Chinese lacquer red, the shed door outside the garden (but visible from inside the garden) is lime green, and portions of the trim on the roof and chimney are cobalt blue. His judicious use of color sets off the predominant green of the potager.

The view looking out from the potager is as handsome as the scene looking in. Dash uses the shapes of the individual plants as part of his overall design.

LIZ AND JACKIE'S GARDEN
SEEKONK, MASSACHUSETTS
(Hardiness Zone 5)

Liz and Jackie's garden is an herb garden approximately 25 feet in diameter with a combination of culinary and medicinal herbs. The pathways are not only for walking on — made of thyme, they are edible as well. Such paths, however, will not stand up to heavy foot traffic. The round beds are set off with concrete bricks. Primarily an herb garden, it provides enough herbs for the household to use fresh and dried for out-of-season use.

Set a distance from the house, the garden requires little or no supplemental water once the plants are established. Most of the herbs are perennial, so the greatest effort is put forth in harvesting rather than in maintenance or planting.

Liz and Jackie's Plant List

Edibles
Anise hyssop
Bee balm
Borage
Calendula
Fennel
Horseradish
Lavender
Marjoram
Mint
Oregano
Perilla
Rosemary
Sages
Sunflower
Thymes

Ornamentals
and Medicinals
Artemisia
Celosia
Feverfew
Globe thistle
Lamb's ears
Sedum

Calendulas

Liz and Jackie's herb potager thrives with only the water that nature provides in summer. Gray foliage plants are especially drought tolerant, as are many of the Mediterranean herbs.

DEBI'S GARDEN, TRANQUIL LAKE NURSERY
REHOBOTH, MASSACHUSETTS
(Hardiness Zone 5)

Tranquil Lake Nursery is one of the largest nurseries specializing in daylilies as well as irises. The range of colors and flavors of the daylilies is remarkable, with every color but blue, pure white, and black represented in the eight acres of growing fields. Daylilies are completely edible — from the new growth in spring (cut the green leaves when they are less than 8 inches long; they're delicious and crispy in stir-fries and salads) to the buds the day before they open (called golden needles, they are a standard ingredient in Chinese hot and sour soup) to the flowers (good cooked or raw; some are very sweet and are excellent when made into a sorbet or used as an edible cup for ice cream or sorbet) to the tubers (dug in fall or winter and used as a substitute for water chestnuts).

Debi's Garden Plant List

Beans
Broccoli
Cilantro
Corn
Eggplants
Marigolds
Moonflowers
Nasturtiums
Peppers
Potatoes
Squashes
Strawberries
Tomatoes
Zucchini

To limit the amount of squash, you can eat the flowers.

The low, bent-twig fence will be covered with moonflowers as the summer continues, and the peppers will fill out the tomato cages.

Debi Hogan created this kitchen garden to complement the daylilies and to be of special interest to children. Making use of a dead tree as a support for vining beans and ornamental moonflowers, she created a hideaway tepee. Corn is grown near the edge of the garden, rather than at the back where it is put traditionally, so that visitors can see how quickly it grows. The positioning also allows Debi to see easily if raccoons are trying to steal the corn. Bentwood arches define the edge of the garden and keep little feet on the path.

PAT LANZA'S GARDEN
LIVINGSTON MANOR, NEW YORK
(Hardiness Zone 3)

Pat Lanza has a very short growing season, located as she is in the Catskill Mountains of New York. She expects at least two frost-free months — July and August, although she has reported snow flurries in late August. Consequently, the herb portion of her kitchen garden is sited against the house for optimum protection for the perennial herbs she grows. Vegetables and annual herbs (the true annuals, such as basil, as well as the herbs she has to grow as annuals, including lavender) are grown in several beds with grass pathways.

'Australian Yellow Leaf' and dark 'Ibis' lettuces are planted in tight rows for a checkerboard look.

Beans climb up a tepee at Pat Lanza's Catskill Mountain garden, providing a strong vertical accent. The cow mural is a whimsical touch painted on the storage barn.

Mediterranean herbs, such as oregano, sage, marjoram, and thyme, like good drainage. Pat Lanza grows them against the porch, where they are also protected from the harsh winds of winter.

In addition, Pat grows various combinations of herbs in containers that she can move around the property to highlight a particular area. Green beans grow up a bamboo tepee, with lavender at the base. The backdrop to the garden is a bucolic bovine mural painted on her barn. Pat grows enough herbs and salad greens to use fresh in the meals she prepares for the numerous visitors to her garden shop and to dry for bouquets and craft projects.

Pat has several greenhouses and grows all her plants from seed. As soon as the weather is warm enough and danger of frost is past, Pat has good-size transplants ready to set out in the garden. An additional challenge is the soil, or lack of it. Pat gardens on hardpan (most of her land is an old hayfield). Over the years she has developed her own method for dealing with this, which she calls lasagna gardening. To create a new bed, she starts in fall by laying about ten sheets of newspaper and a layer of cardboard down on the ground. After thoroughly moistening them, she adds about 2 inches of peat moss. On top of that she puts several inches of compost. Subsequent layers are alternated with peat moss — grass clippings, compostable material, until she reaches a height of about 18 inches. It's all topped with peat moss then left alone for the winter. By spring it's all decomposed and she has about 6 inches of good soil in which to plant. Over time, the organic matter starts to break down the hardpan.

Pat Lanza's Garden Plant List

Basils
Beans: pole and 'Scarlet Runner'
Bee balm
Blanket flower
Chives
Cilantro
Dill
Garlic chives
Gooseneck loosestrife
Kale
Lavender
Lettuces
Marjoram
Mustard
Nasturtiums
Oregano
Pansies
Parsley
Sages
Spinach
Summer savory
Thymes

MATUSON GARDEN
MIAMI, FLORIDA
(Hardiness Zone 10)

This is the most tropical of all the gardens, located in Zone 10. The biggest challenge here was to have some crops that could survive the heat, humidity, and thunderstorms of summer. I consulted on this garden and was soon aware of my lack of knowledge of the heat tolerance of plants. (A heat tolerance zone map for plants is being published by the American Horticultural Society. It will be as helpful for southern gardeners as the cold hardiness zone map is for northern gardeners. At present, only several thousand plants have been rated for heat tolerance, but with the publication of the map, more and more plants that grow in the South will be included.) Many of the herbs that thrive in summer in New York die off by late spring in Florida. The perennial Mediterranean herbs, such

Matuson Garden Plant List

Banana

Basil

Bay

Beans

Broccoli

Carambola (star fruit)

Cauliflower

Eggplant, white

Leeks

Lettuce

Parsley

Peppers

Pineapple

Rosemary

Sage

Sunflowers

Tomatoes

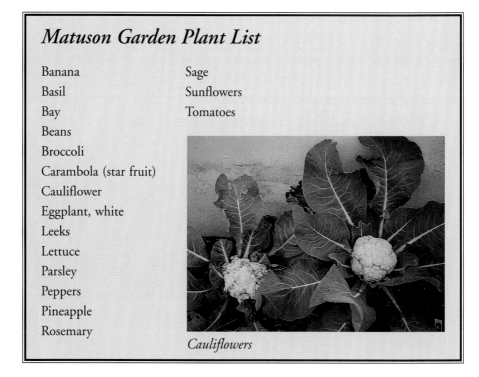

Cauliflowers

Bananas come in a range of sizes to suit any garden — from dwarf varieties only 6 feet tall to magnificent plants that tower 20 feet above the ground.

as rosemary and thyme, which thrive in poor but well-drained soil, are especially problematic. The solution is to grow them as annuals in the cooler months.

Summer is not only a problem for many plants; it is extremely uncomfortable for a person to be out in the garden much after 8 A.M. At the Matuson garden, most of the gardening was done in spring, fall, and winter. Any work that needed to be done in summer was completed, by necessity, by 7 A.M. A path led down the center of the garden; the east side was bordered by the wall of the house; the west side by a 6-foot stucco wall. An attempt at growing some of the herbs between the stepping stones of the path met with only partial success.

Perhaps it was beginner's luck, or the fact that Maria had double-dug the soil and enriched it with plenty of organic matter, but she successfully grew cauliflower and cabbage from seed the first year she put in the garden. Both of these are cool-climate crops, typically grown in the North in spring and fall. When I visited in November, she was harvesting beautiful heads from plants she had sown several months earlier. You definitely know you are not in a temperate garden when you see the star fruit, which grows almost like a weed, and bananas growing side by side with traditional crops.

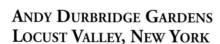

ANDY DURBRIDGE GARDENS
LOCUST VALLEY, NEW YORK
(Hardiness Zone 7)

For many years this garden had been a combination cutting, shrub, and kitchen garden. When Andy Durbridge took it over, he turned it into a unique potager. The single bed is about 30 feet deep and 50 feet long. Flanked by a 3-foot wall on the south side, there are walkways around the other sides of the garden.

The garden was designed with aesthetics first and foremost. The shrubs growing against the wall were left in place; those in the garden itself were moved to other locations on the property. A low-growing border of shrubs, including junipers and euonymus, were installed to anchor the east side of the garden. Three trellises seems to grow out of the shrubs, with a combination of ornamentals and edibles winding their way up — passionflower (both flowers and fruit are edible, if the summer is long and hot enough to produce fruit), black-eyed Susan vine, morning glory, and golden hops.

As Andy and his wife, Donna, often come out to the garden to pick vegetables for dinner late in the day, it was important for them to have some plants for late-day interest. The four o'clocks provide bright color — hot pink, yellow, and white — as well as a haunting fragrance from late afternoon into the night, when the flowers are open. For this reason Andy also chose shrubs with blue-toned or yellowish foliage — dark green leaves disappear at night — as well as variegated varieties of peppers and nasturtiums.

Two wooden tripods with inedible morning glories and 'Scarlet Runner' beans twining upwards provide focal points in the garden. The brilliantly colored 'Heavenly Blue' morning glories are a fine foil for the bright orange 'Scarlet Runner' bean flowers. The lettuces were planted in rows within a triangle — red-leafed varieties alternating with green-leafed ones.

This garden produces food from spring onward, starting with a succession of lettuces that last through the summer. The thinnings from the first planting of beets are eaten as greens. A second planting of carrots and the parsnips are heavily mulched with salt hay in the fall so they can be dug and enjoyed throughout the winter.

Andy Durbridge Garden Plant List

Edibles

Anise hyssop
Basil
Beets
Bush beans
Calendula
Carrots
Chives
Cucumbers
Garlic
Hops
Lavender
Lettuces
Marigold
Melons
Mint
Nasturtiums
Onion
Parsley
Parsnips
Passionflower (passion fruit)
Peppers
Rhubarb
Sage
Salvia
Squashes
Sunflower
Thyme
Tomatoes
Turnips

Ornamentals/Medicinals

Asters
Black-eyed Susan vine
Cleome
Four o'clocks
Mexican sunflowers
Morning glory
Statice

Assorted sweet peppers

'Lemon Boy' tomato is a low-acid tomato with good flavor.

IGLEHART GARDEN
SAINT JAMES, NEW YORK
(Hardiness Zone 6)

I designed this garden for a family of six to provide enough food for fresh eating from late spring to fall as well as freezing and canning for out-of-season use. Each family member was asked what fruits and vegetables he or she liked best, so that the garden would be as practical as possible — no plant was included unless at least three family members like to eat it.

Before the garden was installed, the area, measuring approximately 25 feet on each side, was originally scruffy lawn that was shaded by several insignificant trees. The design is a modern interpretation of a traditional four-square kitchen garden with a center bed. There are five beds; the center one is freeform and the outer four each have at least one straight side (facing the outside of the garden).

Once the design was approved, the entire family pitched in to help create the garden. Everyone helped cut trees down and chip the branches. Once the area was cleared, they used yellow bias tape to lay out the beds. Great loads of well-rotted manure and compost were brought in, and Jackie rototilled it into the beds. Even the smallest child brought loads of compost from the pile to the garden in his Radio Flyer wagon. The grass was turned under, compost, manure, and dolomitic limestone were added to each bed (the soil on Long Island is acidic; lime lowers the pH). The beds ended up about 6 inches higher than the surrounding paths.

The goal was to make a garden that was as attractive as it was practical. Plants were considered for their form and the color and texture of their foliage as well as the color of their fruit (if they produced fruit). The hope was to have enough variety in the garden, using perennials, shrubs, trees, and annual vegetables, to have diversity that would cut down on any pest problems. Also, while slugs had been a problem on the property in the past, they were not in this garden, which may have been due in part to the salt hay.

A bean and pumpkin tepee was constructed of six 8-foot lengths of bamboo lashed together at the top and inserted 6 inches into the ground. We hoped

that the tepee would encourage the youngest child to participate in the garden. In fact, he sat for hours on end in the cool shade of the large leaves in his tepee, watching the rest of the family work. Once the 'Baby Boo' pumpkins began to develop, he was enthralled, watching them each day.

Iglehart Garden Plant List

Anise hyssop
Apple trees, espaliered
Asparagus
Basil 'Spicy Globe'
Beans: pole and green
Blackberries
Borage
Broccoli
Calendulas
Carrots
Cauliflower
Chrysanthemums
Collards
Corn
Cucumbers
Daylilies
Garlic chives
Grapes
Kale
Leeks
Lettuce
Lima beans
Marigold: 'Lemon Gem'
    and 'Tangerine Gem'

Nasturtiums
Onions
Pansies
Pear trees, espaliered
Peas: shelling and edible-
    podded
Peppers: hot and sweet
Pineapple sage
Pinks (Dianthus)
Pinto beans
Pumpkin 'Baby Boo'
Radishes
Raspberries

Sage
Scented geraniums
Squash: yellow and
    butternut
Spinach
Strawberries
Sunflowers (dwarf)
Swiss chard
Tomatoes
Turnip
Yucca
Zucchini

Carrots

A bean tepee is a perfect hidey-hole for any child; from there he can supervise the adults working in the garden. Leave the vines on the supports and the tepee is a magical place even in the snow.

MENGES KITCHEN GARDEN
SHANDELEE, NEW YORK
(Hardiness Zone 4)

Menges Garden Plant List

Basil
Borage
Broccoli
Broccoli raab
Brussels sprouts
Cabbage
Carrots
Cauliflower
Chervil
Chives
Corn
Dill
Eggplant
Egyptian onions
Kale
Lettuce
Marigolds
Mustard greens
Nasturtiums
Parsley
Peppers: hot and sweet
Radishes
Scallions
Tomatoes
Zucchini

This garden was horticultural therapy in action. My friend Steve Menges had used the property for a weekend and holiday retreat after inheriting it from his mother. He had recently been diagnosed as HIV-positive and wanted to live more healthfully, including eating organically grown fruits and vegetables. He planned to take a leave of absence from his job in New York City and live full time on this property. The goal was to create a garden that would begin to produce almost immediately and would cost as little as possible. He also wanted a garden that wouldn't require much maintenance. I designed the garden in a large U shape, with the beds 4 feet wide, so that you could reach any part of the garden without stepping in it.

Since time was a consideration and the only available area for the garden was a hayfield with a very shallow layer of topsoil above a layer of hardpan, I decided that tilling would not be an option. Before we began, we cut the "grass" as short as possible. We used locust logs (cut from the property) about a foot in diameter to define the borders of the garden. Once they were in place, I put down a layer of newspaper ten to fifteen sheets thick, completely covering the grass, then wet it with a hose. On top of that, I placed two layers of cardboard and moistened them. I filled the beds to within an inch of the top of the logs with topsoil, compost, and peat moss, and mixed the soil mix thoroughly with a shovel. I moistened the soil in the beds and let it sit overnight (to allow the peat moss to absorb the moisture). The next morning I began planting — with transplants from my own garden. By the end of the day, the garden was filled with a large variety of vegetables and a few herbs and edible flowers. The next day, after a gentle rain, we

Logs taken from dead trees in Steve Menges' woods form the sides of the raised beds in his garden. Large rocks keep the logs from rolling out of place until they settle (after a season of gardening).

added a 2-inch layer of mulch around all the plants. Within two weeks, Steve was harvesting salad greens. After six weeks, he was eating tomatoes, basil, peppers, eggplants, and the rest of the bounty of the garden. The only maintenance was watering the garden every third day, as the weather was extremely hot and dry. A fence was added the second season to keep rabbits and deer away from the garden.

BARASH EDIBLE FLOWER GARDEN
COLD SPRING HARBOR, NEW YORK
(Hardiness Zone 7)

This Long Island garden was conceived in 1991 when I started writing a book on edible flowers. It is made up exclusively of plants with edible blooms. The one plant that was a partial compromise was a cut-leaf Japanese maple; although maple flowers are edible, they are neither very tasty nor has their safety been ascertained, so they were not included in my book. The tree was such a beautiful anchor for the garden, especially in winter when decorated with white fairy lights. However, it succumbed to a blight, and a native redbud (with bright pink, pea-flavored, crunchy flowers in spring) was put in its place.

A pie-wedge-shaped garden with a radius of 15 feet, it packs a lot of plants in a small space. Gardening with such limitations, I try to layer plants so that the same space may be filled by two or more plants as the year progresses. For example, in spring tulips bloom in an array of colors throughout the garden. The ripening foliage of these bulbs is hidden by the emerging leaves of the daylilies, which flower in summer.

From the earliest tulips in spring to the chrysanthemums of fall, there are flowers in bloom in this garden at least eight months of the year. One trick I recently learned is to include fall-planted pansies. Even in a severe winter, when we had 2 feet of snow and ice that began to resemble a glacier, when the ice melted in late January, there were the pansies, blooming their hearts out.

Like many gardeners, I like to stretch the limits of the plants I can grow. Two tropical plants were cornerstones of this garden — jasmine and pineapple sage. The jasmine was in a 10-inch hanging basket and was easily brought outside after the last spring frost and back inside before the first chill of autumn. Pineapple sage, my favorite edible flower (its flavor is like a ripe papaya), grows to a small tree. It was worth lugging it in and out with the seasons — the flowers, indoors in April and often a second bloom outdoors in August, were unsurpassable.

Stepping stones lead to the compost pile, which is well hidden behind the roses in my edible flower garden. In late spring the garden abounds with bloom: (clockwise from bottom) Johnny-jump-ups, coriander, nasturtiums, cleome, 'Lemon Gem' marigold, roses, chamomile, 'Scarlet Runner' beans, and calendulas.

Barash Garden Plant List

Anise hyssop
Apple
Arugula
Basils
Bee balm
Borage
Broccoli
Calendula
Chamomile
Chicory
Chives
Chrysanthemums
Cilantro (coriander)
Dandelion
Daylilies
Dianthus
Dill
Elderflower (elderberry)

English daisy
Garlic chives
Hollyhocks
Honeysuckle
Jasmine
Johnny-jump-ups
Lavender
Lilacs
Lilies
Marigolds
Marjoram
Nasturtiums
Nodding onion
Oregano
Pansies
Peas
Pineapple guava
Pineapple sage

Radish
Redbud
Red clover
Rosemary
Rose of Sharon
Roses: 'Gertrude Jekyll',
    rugosa roses, *R. rubrifolia*
Scarlet runner bean
Scented geraniums
Society garlic
Summer savory
Sweet woodruff
Thymes
Tuberous begonias
Tulips
Violets
Winter savory
Yucca

Johnny-jump-ups

BALL GARDEN
SPRINGFIELD, PENNSYLVANIA
(Hardiness Zone 6)

This raised-bed kitchen garden is a modular design so that a variety of modifications can be made to any single bed with a minimum of work. For example, there are couplings that allow trellises or PVC hoops to be added to the bed. The trellises allow tomatoes, pole beans, cucumbers, and peas to grow vertically, thus maximizing the use of bed space. The hoops are installed in spring or fall and a spun-fabric cloth is draped over them to extend the growing season. In spring, the fabric helps to warm the beds, allowing for an earlier planting; in fall it keeps frost from salad greens. The fabric, when placed early enough over

Ball Garden Plant List

Basil
Beans
Beets
Carrots
Cucumbers
Grapes
Kiwi
Lettuces
Nasturtiums
Pansies
Peas: podded and sugar snap
Peppers: hot and sweet
Radishes
Raspberries
Tomatillos
Tomatoes

Hot peppers

Guy wires help to stabilize the trellises as they are laden with vines, planted on both sides. This allows for twice the harvest and easy picking.

the beds, helps to deter leaf miners from chard and spinach and borers and other pests from reaching the squash and cucumbers. However, the fabric must be removed when the squash and cucumbers begin to bloom, or none of the pollinating insects can get to the flowers.

Peas are planted on both sides of the center trellis for twice the harvest in the same space. Virginia sweetspire adds evening interest with its cascading white flowers.

After several years, some of the trellises were replaced with a permanent grape and hardy kiwi arbor. The trellises simply weren't strong enough for the prolific grapes and kiwis, and an arbor was a much more attractive feature in the winter when it was bare.

STEVEN RUCE'S HELIOTROPE GARDENS
ORONO, MINNESOTA
(Hardiness Zone 4)

Steven Ruce's garden has perhaps the most demanding climate challenges of all the gardens we will examine. Located on a hillside outside of Minneapolis, this garden is terraced. The beds are not raised but level with each of the concrete terraces. The concrete absorbs the sun's heat in the spring and transfers the heat to the beds, so they are plantable before the surrounding countryside.

Several of the beds are made to be used as cold frames, with raised wooden

The A-frame supports are strung in the center to allow pole bean 'Gold Marie' to twine upward. Under the beans are lettuces, which are cooled from the hot summer sun by the beans' foliage.

A-frame supports are sturdy enough to hold a half dozen tomato plants at Steven Ruce's Heliotrope Gardens. Despite the fruits' diminutive size, both 'Black Plum' and 'Matt's Wild Cherry' are among the most flavorful tomatoes.

sides and removable lids. Several beds have a heater cable in them so that even with the severe Zone 4 winters, Ruce can have salad greens all year long. (He won't admit what the cost of raising these greens in heated conditions in subzero weather is, however.) The beds are fitted with an irrigation system so that the plants are watered at soil level.

Deer are a problem in the area, and on the rest of the property they graze as they wish. When I visited the garden, bars of soap had been placed in several of the beds as a deterrent; tooth marks, however, indicated that the deer just ate the

Heliotrope Gardens Plant List

Edibles
Basils
Beets
Broccoli 'Green Goliath'
Chard 'Ruby'
Daylily 'Bittersweet Honey'
Eggplant
Fennel 'Bronze'
Lettuces
Onion 'Egyptian Multiplier'
Parsley
Pea 'Knight'
Pepper 'Pretty Purple'
Pole bean 'Gold Marie'
Rose 'Hansa'
Salad burnet
Spinach 'Bloomsdale Longstanding'
Strawberry 'Ozark Beauty'
Tomatoes: 'Black Plum', 'Matt's
    Wild Cherry', and 'Stakeless F'

Ornamentals
Nicotiana (flowering tobacco)
Snapdragons
Zinnias

Snapdragons

The stone that surrounds Steve Ruce's garden helps to warm the soil in the beds early in the season — an important plus in a Zone 4 garden.

soap. Another bed that was newly planted with peas had wire supports zigzagging across it to deter would-be nibblers. The deer are less problematic in the kitchen gardens; Ruce surmises that they are deterred by the concrete.

This garden makes the best possible use of the space available, with tomatoes, beans, and cucumbers trained to A-frame trellises placed in some of the beds. Greens, like lettuce and spinach, which prefer cool weather, are planted in these beds early and are then shaded by the heat-loving vines.

KUHLMAN GARDEN
CENTER MORICHES, NEW YORK
(Hardiness Zone 6)

After many years of growing most of their vegetables in a single large bed, with the inherent drainage, weeding, and soil compaction problems, Susan and Jay Kuhlman decided to create a kitchen garden with 12 raised beds. An added benefit was that the dogs did not dash through the raised beds the way they had in the flat garden, so they no longer damaged the plants.

An avid tomato enthusiast, Jay grows 28 different varieties of tomatoes (one plant of each), including many heirloom varieties from Europe. The harvest is

Kuhlman Garden Plant List

Arugula
Basils
Fava beans
Fig (at edge of garden)
Lettuces
Mâche
Mustard
Nasturtiums
Pear (at edge of garden)
Peppers
Pole beans
Ramp
Rhubarb
Spinach
Squash
Sugar snap peas
Tomatoes

Better Boy Tomato

Susan Kuhlman wastes no time in the spring; as soon as her husband Jay finishes making the new raised beds, she fills the beds with a mixture of soil and compost and then plants them.

enormous, partly due to all the organic matter incorporated into the soil when the beds were created, just prior to planting the tomatoes. The Kuhlmans live in an area where they can get free compost from their township, and they take full advantage of that service.

Jay has always grown a good range of dahlias for cut flowers. These, too, benefited from their new location. A squash (grown from seeds bought on an Italian vacation) ran rampant over the garden, eventually surrounding all the beds. Again, the organic matter in the soil promoted plant growth — perhaps a little too well.

HARDINESS ZONE MAP

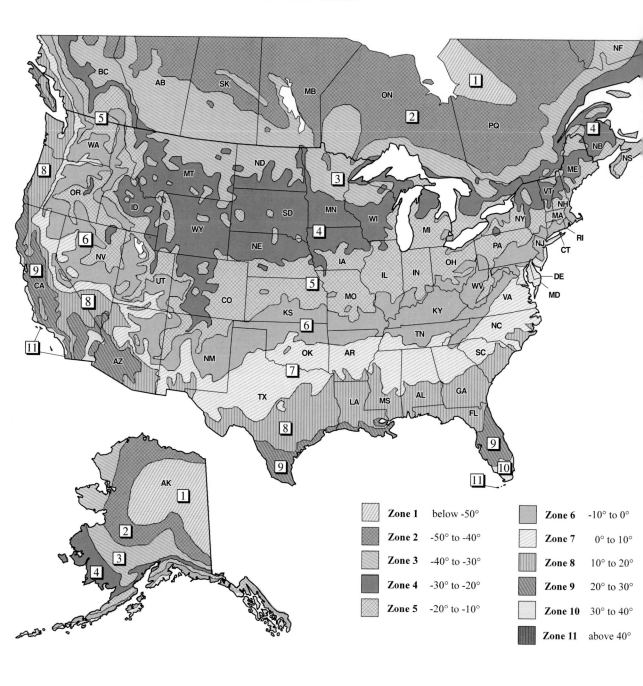

Zone 1	below -50°	Zone 6	-10° to 0°
Zone 2	-50° to -40°	Zone 7	0° to 10°
Zone 3	-40° to -30°	Zone 8	10° to 20°
Zone 4	-30° to -20°	Zone 9	20° to 30°
Zone 5	-20° to -10°	Zone 10	30° to 40°
		Zone 11	above 40°

APPENDIX 1:
SEED VIABILITY

Vegetable	Number of years seed should be viable
Beans	3
Beets	6
Broccoli	4
Brussels sprouts	4
Cabbage	4
Carrot	2
Cauliflower	4
Celery	2
Corn	5
Cucumber	6
Eggplant	4
Lettuce	6
Onion	3
Peas	3
Peppers	4
Pumpkin	4
Radish	4
Spinach	3
Squash	4
Swiss chard	6
Tomatoes	6

APPENDIX 2:
EXPECTED YIELD OF COMMON VEGETABLES

Vegetable	Pounds yielded per 10 feet of row
Asparagus	2 to 4
Beans, bush	5 to 10
Beans, pole	15 to 20
Beets	8 to 12
Broccoli	8 to 10
Brussels sprouts	4 to 6
Cabbage	15 to 20
Cabbage, Chinese	6 to 10
Carrots	8 to 10
Cauliflower	8 to 10
Celery	50 to 100 stalks
Corn	10 to 15 ears
Cucumbers	10 to 15
Eggplants	5 to 10
Lettuce, head	10 to 12 heads
Lettuce, leaf	4 to 8
Onions	4 to 8
Peas, edible podded	7 to 12
Peas, shelling	2 to 5 (shelled)
Peppers	25 to 40 peppers
Potatoes	10 to 15
Pumpkins	15 to 150
Radishes	5 to 10
Rhubarb	8 to 12
Spinach	3 to 5
Squash, summer	10 to 15
Squash, winter	15 to 25
Swiss chard	10 to 20
Tomatoes	10 to 25

APPENDIX 3:
TEMPERATURES FOR GERMINATION AND GROWING VEGETABLES

Plant	Temp. for Germination (Degrees F.)	Germination Time (Days)	Temp. for Growing (Degrees F.)	Weeks until Ready to Transplant
Broccoli	45°–85°	4–12	55°–75°	4–6
Brussels sprouts	45°–85°	4–12	55°–75°	4–6
Cabbage	45°–95°	4–12	55°–75°	4–6
Cauliflower	45°–85°	4–12	55°–75°	4–6
Celeriac	60°–70°	7–14	55°–75°	10–12
Eggplant	75°–90°	7–14	65°–85°	8–10
Leeks	50°–95°	7–14	55°–75°	6–8
Lettuce	40°–80°	2–14	55°–75°	2–4
Onions	50°–95°	7–14	55°–75°	6–8
Parsley	50°–85°	14–28	55°–75°	10–12
Peppers	65°–85°	7–14	65°–85°	8–10
Tomatoes	60°–85°	7–14	55°–85°	6–8

All the numbers in this chart are ranges, as there are so many variables that can affect germination times. Temperature can also be dependent on relative moisture and light.

Appendix 4:
Best Storage Methods for Your Harvest

Depending on your time and energy at harvest time, these are the best short-
and long-term options for storing your garden produce.

Plant	Wash	Store short term/long term	Ideal humidity/temperature
Artichoke	A	I/C	Moist/cold
Asparagus	A	I/C, F	
Basil	A	RT/F, D	
Beans, shell or dry	—	I/D, C, F	
Beans, green	A	I/F, C, D	
Beets	A	I/RC, F, C	Moist/cold
Berries	B	I/F, C, D	
Broccoli	A	I/F, C, RCP	Moist/cold
Brussels sprouts	A	I/F, RC (short term)	Moist/cold
Cabbage	A	I/C (sauerkraut), RC (short term)	Moist/cold
Cantaloupe	A	I	
Carrots	A	I/F, C, D, RC	Moist/cold
Cauliflower	A	I/F, C, RC, RCP	Moist/cold

KEY:

B — Wash gently before storing
A — Wash after storing and before eating, cooking, or processing
I — Refrigerate
F — Freeze
C — Can
D — Dry (dehydrator, oven, or air dry)
RC — Root cellar
RCP — Root cellar potted
(Dig plant up, replant in 1- to 5-gallon pot, and store in root cellar until ready to eat. Keep lightly moist.)
RT — Room temperature

Moist/cold — 90 to 95 percent humidity at 32 to 34° F.

Moist/cool — 85 to 90 percent humidity.
    Potatoes: 38 to 40°F.
    Melons and peppers: 45° to 50° F.
    Tomatoes and sweet potatoes: 55° to 65° F.

Dry/cold — 65 percent humidity at 32° to 34° F.

Dry/cool — 65 percent humidity at 35° to 50° F
    (except for winter squash and pumpkins, which prefer 70 percent humidity at 55° F.

Plant	Wash	Store short term/long term	Ideal humidity/temperature
Chicory	A	I/RC (when forcing for Belgian endive)	Moist/cold
Collards	B	I/F, C, RCP	Moist/cold
Corn	A	I/F, C, D	Dry/cold (for dried corn)
Cucumber	B	I/C (pickles)	
Currants	B	I/F, D, C (jelly)	
Dill	B	I/F, D	
Edible flowers	B	I (briefly)/D	
Eggplant	A	I (50°F is ideal)/F	
Endive	B	I/RC (short term), RCP	Moist/cold
Escarole	B	I/RC (short term), RCP	Moist/cold
Fennel	A	I/F, D	
Garlic	A	RT/I, R, RC	Dry/cold
Horseradish	B	I/F, C, RC	Moist/cold
Jerusalem artichoke	A	I/I, RC	Moist/cold
Kale	B	I/F, C, RCP	Moist/cold
Kohlrabi	B	I/RC (short term), RCP	Moist/cold
Leeks	A	I/F, D, RC	Moist/cold
Lettuce	B	I/ RCP	Moist/cold
Mustard greens	B	I/F	
Okra	A	I/F, D	
Onions	A	I/F, C, D, RC	Dry/cold
Oregano/marjoram	A	I/F, D	
Parsnips	A	I/F, RC	Moist/cold
Peas			
Edible podded	A	I/F	
Shelling	A	I/F, C, D	
Peppers	A	I/F, C, D	
Potatoes	A	I/F (only if precooked or shredded), RC	Moist/cold

Plant	Wash	Store short term/long term	Ideal humidity/temperature
Radishes	A	I/RC	Moist/cold
Rhubarb	B	I/F, C	
Sage	A	I/F, D	
Salsify	A	I/F, RC	Moist/cold
Sorrel	A	I/F (pureed)	
Soybeans	A	I/F (when still green), D	
Spinach	B	I/F, RCP	Moist/cold
Squash			
summer	A	R/F (pureed, chopped, or shredded)	
winter	A	RT, I (when cut)/F (cooked), C (cooked), RC	Dry/cold
Sweet potatoes	A	RT, I/F (if cooked), C, RC	Moist/cold
Swiss chard	B	I/F, C	
Thyme	A	I/F, D	
Tomatoes	A	I (only if ripe)/F, C, D, RC (green or long-keepers only)	Moist/cold
Turnips	A	I/F, RC	Moist/cold
Watermelon	A	RT, I/I, F (if very ripe)	

Key:

B — Wash gently before storing

A — Wash after storing and before eating, cooking, or processing

I — Refrigerate

F — Freeze

C — Can

D — Dry (dehydrator, oven, or air dry)

RC — Root cellar

RCP — Root cellar potted

(Dig plant up, replant in 1- to 5-gallon pot, and store in root cellar until ready to eat. Keep lightly moist.)

RT — Room temperature

Moist/cold — 90 to 95 percent humidity at 32 to 34° F.

Moist/cool — 85 to 90 percent humidity.
    Potatoes: 38 to 40°F.
    Melons and peppers: 45° to 50° F.
    Tomatoes and sweet potatoes: 55° to 65° F.

Dry/cold — 65 percent humidity at 32° to 34° F.

Dry/cool — 65 percent humidity at 35° to 50° F
    (except for winter squash and pumpkins,
    which prefer 70 percent humidity at 55° F.

PHOTO CREDITS

INDEX

Page numbers in italics refer to illustrations.

Titles available in the Taylor's Weekend Gardening Guides series:

Organic Pest and Disease Control	$12.95
Safe and Easy Lawn Care	12.95
Window Boxes	12.95
Attracting Birds and Butterflies	12.95
Water Gardens	12.95
Easy, Practical Pruning	12.95
The Winter Garden	12.95
Backyard Building Projects	12.95
Indoor Gardens	12.95
Plants for Problem Places	12.95
Soil and Composting	12.95
Kitchen Gardens	12.95
Garden Paths	12.95
Easy Plant Propagation	12.95

At your bookstore or by calling 1-800-225-3362

Prices subject to change without notice